Quilted Clothing

Quilted Clothing

By Jean Ray Laury

Oxmoor House, Inc. · Birmingham

Copyright© 1982 Oxmoor House, Inc.
Book Division of Southern Progress Corporation
P.O. Box 2463, Birmingham, Alabama 35201

Library of Congress Catalog Number: 81-80139
ISBN: 0-8487-0526-2
Manufactured in the United States of America
First Printing 1982

ISBN 0-8487-0526-2

Contents

Imagine yourself snuggled into a quilt on a chilly evening, luxuriating in the inviting texture of quilted fabric. Draping the quilt around yourself, you may wonder if you couldn't snip here, fold and cut there, and make a garment—in short, wear the quilt. Quilted garments feel wonderful. They are like comforters made to fit *people* instead of beds. But that is just part of the reason so many women are making them. Quilted clothes also tend to be joyous. A beautiful garment has a magic quality; it can cast a spell on a whole room, transporting wearer and viewer alike. Along with being comfortable and magical, there is an element of practicality to making your own clothes. Quilted clothing offers relatively lightweight warmth for outdoor activities, and with thermostats down, quilted clothes provide coziness and comfort along with beauty for indoor use.

The transition from quilts to quilted clothing is a direct one, carrying with it the techniques of traditional quiltmakers. Many of the designers whose work is included here came to clothing design through quilt making. A few have actually cut up their own quilts (or old ones) to make the most direct transition! The current passion for handmade clothes is one inevitable result of our increased appreciation for quilts.

The title *Quilted Clothing* makes generous and broad use of both the title words. "Quilted" is taken to refer not only to the quilting process itself, but to methods traditionally used in quilting: padding, piecing, patchwork, strip quilting, appliqué, and trapunto. In a larger sense, "quilting" carries the connotation of a folk art, bringing to mind the handmade quality of personally designed and colorfully adorned pieces of work.

"Clothing" refers in an obvious way to garments, such as vests, coats, and jackets, and to ethnic clothes as well. Ethnic clothes, more respected and appreciated than ever before, add variety to our choice of styles. A few aprons, boots, and bags are brought into the book.

Folk costumes from around the world have earned our respect and helped us to appreciate artistic merit in clothing. These designs have endured because of their ingenious use of material, the simple way in which they fold and stack, and their sophisticated use of color and pattern. We are learning, too, that clothes of great integrity can be worn for years and passed from one person to another. Economic needs have long demanded the qualities of durability and beauty in many ethnic garments. Our own economic and energy needs now support a similar approach.

Wear and tear and the moth have combined to leave us with scant evidence of the antiquity of the quilting technique. Historical records indicate that quilted clothing was at first the province of the wealthy and aristocratic. It didn't take others long to see the advantages for themselves in those padded layers. Soon warm, durable quilted clothes were constructed for work, even when it was necessary to unravel pieces of cast-off clothing to get wool for padding. The first armor was simply a padded, quilted garment. When newer weaponry rendered quilted armor ineffective, it was still worn under chain mail and plate metal to ease the discomfort. Some 3000 years ago, an Egyptian king wore a quilted cloak with his crown. Chaucer describes his knight's quilted armor in great detail. Household inventories of medieval castles and mansions saw fit to list among family treasures quilted bedding and clothing. The richly detailed and beautifully constructed garments shown in this book are also worthy of such lists of personal treasures.

The collection of garments in this book is a tribute to women who sew. Some of these women are artists; some are home-sewers. All are designers, and all shape an interest in producing works that are of lasting quality. Their work indicates a concern for the beauty and function of the garment as well as pleasure in producing it.

It is the purpose of this book to help you in two ways: First, to offer you a showcase of clothing ideas that will inspire you and stimulate your imagination. Second, to provide you with patterns, directions, and details for some of the garments you are encouraged to make your own. The book shares with you the creative possibilities of quilted clothing design. The examples involve wholesome and imaginative, sometimes humorous, and always human, approaches to clothing. *Quilted Clothing* offers encouragement to the beginner, inspiration to the more experienced, and the possibility of pleasure for all.

Making Your Garment

SELECTING & ADAPTING A PATTERN

Simple patterns are most easily adapted to quilting and patchwork. The complexities of darts, gussets, or fitted bodices should be avoided, especially by the beginner. A pattern with straight lines will simplify your work, whereas gathers, pleats, or ruffles are difficult to adapt. Lapels can be a problem, since the thickness of the layers adds bulk that tends to make lapels stand out instead of lying flat. Browsing through this book will give you a good idea of the types of patterns that work most successfully.

Since ethnic patterns are so often made from simple strips of fabric, they are perfect for quilting and piecing techniques. Many of the garments in this book were made from two particular pattern sources. One is Folkwear, a company that makes a variety of patterns that are based on traditional ethnic garments. Another excellent source is Yvonne Porcella's self-published book called *Pieced Clothing* with patterns given by diagram. These two wellsprings of inspiration have prompted numerous glorious garments, many of which are presented here. At the end of this book, under References, page 150, you will find these and other pattern makers and companies with patterns that are adapted from folk and ethnic costumes.

Many commercial patterns also adapt well to appliqué and patchwork. You should consider both the type of embellishment you will use and whether you intend to quilt the garment when you make your selection. If the pattern you have selected is made for quilted clothes, it will usually tell you how much allowance is already given. On a jacket pattern, ease will have been added, so that the garment will slip over other clothes.

If you are using a pattern that you intend to adapt to quilting, you will need to add enough extra material to each pattern to allow for the bulk of the padding as well as for what will be drawn up in the quilting stitches. Generally allow about 1″ of extra material for each 8″ of the pattern, or about 2″ on a garment front or back, for quilting and padding. To convert a pattern to the necessary size for a quilted garment, add the following:

  bust: 3″ to 4″
  shoulder length: ½″ to 1″
  arm length: 1″ to 2″
  across back: 2″ to 3″

If you are uncertain about size, make a muslin or scrap fabric shell, baste in a filler and lining, and check size.

To be certain that enough extra fabric is allowed for drawing up into the quilting stitches, many designers prefer to complete the quilting before cutting out the final pattern shape. To do this, cut the fabric approximately 2″ larger than the pattern, place it over your filler and backing, and quilt it according to the instructions under Quilting Garments, page 24. Then cut the garment parts from the prequilted fabric.

SELECTING MATERIALS

Practical aspects need to be considered in selecting your materials: durability, compatibility of various materials, the ease with which they can be hand or machine sewn and quilted, or whether these considerations apply to your project. Of even greater interest is the visual appeal of your selections: color, texture, and pattern.

To make sewing easier, select fabrics having a consistent fiber content. Using all cotton fabric, or all cotton and polyester combinations, will give you the smoothest seams. But you may want to use unlike materials to give a garment richness; a velour yoke, a satin ribbon, or a band of shiny rayon may make your work less practical but more gorgeous. It will be important for you to make the decision of how the garment is to be washed or if you are willing to take on the added expense and a trek to the cleaners.

If the garment is to be machine washable, be sure to run all fabrics through a complete wash cycle before cutting any pattern parts. Remember that top fabric, filler, and backing must all three be washable if you are to have a garment that is washable.

Some smooth-finished fabrics (chintz, glazed cotton, satins) give a special effect when quilted. Because of the sheen of the fabric, the quilting will make a more prominent pattern. This quality is sometimes the basis for a decision to dry clean in order to preserve the glaze for a longer period of time.

Many fabrics can be hand or machine quilted with ease, though a tightly woven fabric will be hard to quilt by hand. A very stiff or heavy-bodied fabric, like sailcloth or heavy sports cotton, will not quilt well by hand or machine. If you are uncertain about the adaptability of any fabric for quilting, quilt a small section of it before committing it to the entire garment.

COLOR & DESIGN

The design of a garment is a composition; color, texture, pattern, borders, and closures combine to form a complete unit. A theme or a central idea or color can give the design a cohesive quality. Selecting components to make a harmonious whole is always the hardest part of the decision making. Harmony can be achieved by relating the different design elements in your garment. Color combinations are one obvious way; textural combinations are another. The color wheel indicates only one aspect of color—hue. Value and intensity are equally important. The most subtle, and often the richest, combinations of colors are those that are closely related to one another—close in hue, value, or intensity.

Contrast refers to the basic differences between colors. These differences offer dramatic effect and activity to a garment. The most extreme example is black and white. The striped black and white bands of the convict's suit give maximum visibility through contrast. Camouflage cloth uses low contrast for the opposite effect of concealment.

Textures can be combined to give a compatibility or a sense of belonging together. The textures can be visual (as with prints) or they can result from the weave, or structure, of the material. Satin, corduroy, and dotted swiss all have textures that are inherent to their structures.

To achieve harmony through textural combinations, try using velours, corduroys, or velveteens together. A collection of cotton prints might be combined in one garment, offering a flower-garden array of colors and patterns. Satins, silks, and ribbons offer a compatible collection of sheens and shiny surfaces. Contrasts in textures (such as satin used with corduroy) create a different and interesting effect.

Visual textures offer tremendous possibilities. Stripes, for example, usually combine two or more contrasting colors. But if the stripes are narrow, the colors will visually mix. For example, a red and white stripe will blend visually to produce pink. Prints are commonly used in garments to provide allover pattern and color. They should be looked at from the vantage point of a little distance to see how they'll "read."

In designing and planning your garment, lay out the fabrics you plan to use. Place them together in the proportions in which you intend to use them. View them from a distance as well as up close. Start with your preferences—then be adventuresome. Begin with what you like and then push the boundaries a little and you will find that color and texture can be exciting parts of the composition.

LININGS

● *Backing as lining*

When three layers of material (top, filler and backing) are placed together for quilting, the bottom layer (or backing) will show the pattern of the quilting. You can use this to advantage as the lining of your garment, particularly in a coat, jacket, or vest where the inside is seen when the garment is open.

When a printed fabric is used for the backing, the quilting stitches can be de-emphasized or concealed (an advantage if your stitches are not too even). A backing in a solid color will give a relief effect as the stitches make patterns on the fabric. Sometimes the quilted lining can be used as a reversible side, so it is possible to have a pieced and a quilted garment in one.

To utilize the quilted backing as a really attractive lining, it will be important to finish all seams and to bind all edges. They may be finished by using any of the methods given in Bindings & Edgings and in Seam Finishes, page 8.

● *Separate lining*

If you do not wish to finish all inside seams, make a separate lining for the garment. This will prevent any exposed batting from showing.

The color or pattern of your lining is important. The lining can complement or highlight the garment. A brilliantly contrasting color is great for lining; since it only occasionally shows, you can be daring and adventuresome with color.

A smooth fabric, such as satin, silk, taffeta, or a standard lining material, will work well. You must decide whether or not you need a washable fabric. Choose one that allows you to slide easily into or out of the garment. This is most important with a coat or jacket that will be pulled on over other clothing. Muslin or printed calico may make a good lining, and printed or patterned materials will add further dimension to your work.

Many commercial garment patterns offer directions for lining. If yours does not, simply use the major pattern pieces for the lining pattern and eliminate the facings. Cut a lining, using the major pattern parts, and join the seams according to the directions for the garment. The linings for quilted clothes need to be made just slightly smaller than the clothes themselves. If you use the same pattern, you can compensate for the size difference by taking just slightly larger seams on the lining. Join the lining to the garment by one of the following methods.

Any lining can be kept in place by binding the edges of garment and lining together. Join the lining pieces, turn the lining inside out, and slip the lining inside the garment. Then baste lining to garment at all open edges. Check at this point to be sure the fit is correct. Then bind the raw edges of the two fabrics according to directions given under Bindings & Edgings.

Linings can also be attached to your garment by slipping them under facings and tacking in place by hand.

Another way of finishing the lined garment is to slip the lining into the garment and baste about 1″ from all outside edges. Then fold raw edges of both garment fabric and lining to the inside so that folded edges can be stitched together. Slip-stitch by hand or topstitch by machine.

To give a knife-edged finish to a lined vest or jacket, place the assembled lining and garment with right sides facing. Stitch on the seam allowance all around neckline, front, and bottom edges. Trim corners and clip curves. Turn the lining to the inside and press, and you have a smooth, flat, finished knife edge. Armholes or sleeves will have to be sewn by hand or topstitched by machine. Do not sew all lining seams, or you will have no way to right the garment.

BINDINGS & EDGINGS

The bindings or edgings on quilted clothes make a great contribution to the overall design. Because they are so important to the design of the garment, it is a good idea to consider edgings as you plan the garment. Bindings can be used as the single most important decorative aspect of a jacket, or they can emphasize a particular color in a dress. Bindings can also be kept very low-key, using colors to match the garments and contrast with the lining so that they show only when the garment is open.

Besides playing this visual role, bindings also offer a simple means of finishing clothes. Because of the bulk of quilted materials, hemming is often not practical or even possible. Bindings, therefore, take on special significance.

The binding or the edging on your garment will be determined first of all by the construction method you have used: whether the piece is quilted or unquilted, whether it is lined or unlined. Our first consideration will be binding for clothes that are quilted. Here, bulk is a factor, and there are several simple means of providing a finished edge.

● *Self Binding*

For a self binding, quilting stitches should be taken only to the seam lines of the garment. There are two kinds of self binding.

In the first kind, the outside garment material will make its own binding. Trim away backing and batting, and fold the garment material over their raw edges. Turn under cut edge of the extending fabric, and slip-stitch. (Figure 1.)

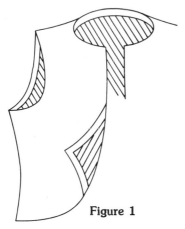

Figure 1

Another method of self binding uses the reverse of this process. Trim away filler and outside fabric so backing material folds over batting and outside material to become the binding on the front of the garment. (Figure 2.)

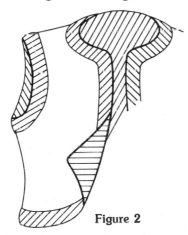

Figure 2

If additional decorative effect is desired, use a ribbon, braid, or cording over the finishing seam on either the lining or the outer garment. (Figure

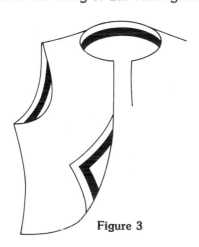

Figure 3

3.) Try a bias strip of printed fabric for zest and contrast, perhaps a print used in the garment. Even a single-fold bias tape in a solid color adds a very snappy touch.

● *Bias Binding*

A quick and effective method of binding involves the use of a bias strip that covers the raw seam edge, as illustrated by the velvet Bird Vest, page 146. In this process, quilting stitches can go all the way to the edge. (In some instances, the decision of how to bind may be determined by whether your quilting stitches stop at the seam lines or extend to the cut edge of your fabric!)

To finish with a binding that is ½″ wide, you will need to cut a bias strip twice that width, plus seam allowances. By cutting a bias 1½″ wide, you will have two ¼″ seam allowances and a ½″-wide finished binding. Adjust width for narrower or wider bindings.

For a long, continuous strip, find the true bias of a rectangular piece of fabric by folding down the crosswise edge of the fabric and aligning it with the lengthwise edge. Crease the fold. Cut along this true bias line and discard the triangle. With a pencil or chalk, mark lines parallel with the true bias line and as wide as you want the strip to be, including seam allowances. (Figure 1.) Form a tube by bringing right sides together, offsetting

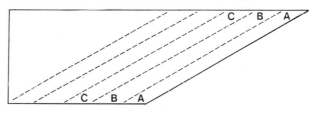

Figure 1

the marked sections, so A meets B, B meets C, etc. Stitch edges together with a ¼″ seam, and press seam open. (Figure 2.) Cut along the lines in a long, continuous strip.

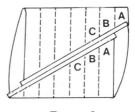

Figure 2

To bind a raw seam, trim the seam allowance of your quilted garment to fit inside the finished width of the bias strip. With right side of bias strip facing the outside of the garment, match seam lines and stitch. (Figure 3.) Turn bias strip to

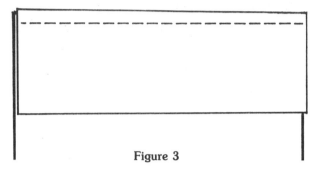

Figure 3

inside so that half of finished bias strip will show outside of garment. Fold under raw edge, and slip-stitch in place. (Figure 4.) For unlimited possi-

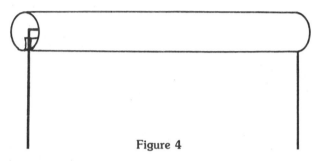

Figure 4

bilities in introducing new patterns and colors, try bias strips of prints, contrasting patterns, and bright, bold colors.

Bias strips can be eased around curves with little difficulty, although a sharp corner may require careful attention. You may prefer to overlap the corner. (Figure 5.) Then trim the excess, tuck

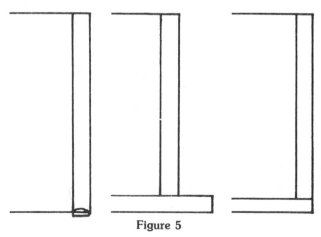

Figure 5

it under, and hand stitch. The African Shirt, page 96, is finished with this type of sharp, squared corner.

To attach a bias binding entirely by machine, first sew the bias strip to the inside of the garment edge. Then fold the bias over the raw seam, turning edge of bias under, and baste to outside of garment. Then topstitch with a row of straight stitches on the outside.

● *Pieced Bindings*

A collection of colors and patterns can be pieced to make unusual bindings. As bias or straight-cut strips, they can form a linear, decorative pattern, picking up and exaggerating colors from a garment. (Figure 6.) In the photograph of

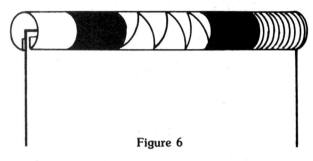

Figure 6

the Black Kimono on page 71, striped materials form a ready-to-go binding of this type.

● *Stuffed Bindings*

For a full, rounded, and comfortably puffy binding such as in the Pieced Jacket, page 55, add batting inside the strip of bias binding. Cut the bias binding a little wider than for its unstuffed counterpart. Sew one edge to the seam allowance of the garment, as in the directions for bias binding, but before slip stitching the binding shut, place a strip of batting along the fold of the fabric. If you are using a bonded batt, cut a strip and roll it (lengthwise) into the binding. (Figure 7.) An

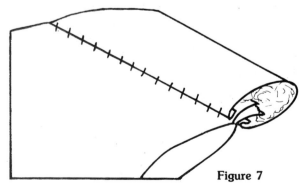

Figure 7

unbonded batt can be pulled into a rope and laid on the bias strip before it is sewn down.

● *Piping*

A piped edge adds an elegant touch to any garment. Piping can be purchased ready-made, but to repeat a specific fabric used in your garment, it will be necessary to make your own. Make a 1½"-wide continuous bias strip as described in Bias Binding, page 5. Fold the bias in half lengthwise, wrong sides together. Place a length of cording in the fold. Using a zipper foot, stitch right next to the cording to make a smooth, firm piping. (Figure 8.) Do not trim off any of the

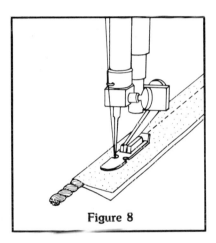

Figure 8

excess fabric; it will be inserted into a seam to secure the piping.

To sew the piping into the seam of the garment, place the piping on the right side of the garment, raw edges aligned. Using a zipper foot, stitch the piping in place. To join other garment parts, lining, or facing, place right sides together and align seam allowances. Turn so garment piece with piping seam is on top. Sew through all thicknesses, again using a zipper foot, slightly to the inside of the first stitching line. Trim if necessary to reduce bulk; it may also be necessary to clip the seam allowances of the piping around outside curves and sharp corners.

● *Facings*

A common finishing method for an unquilted garment is to cut facings for all unfinished outside edges. For example, on a vest, the armhole would need facing, as would the neckline, front, and bottom edges. Cut the facings at least 1½"

wide, following the contours of your garment or pattern pieces. (The cut is indicated by the bro-

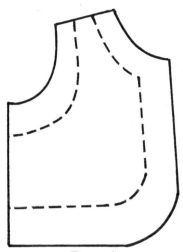

Figure 1

ken line on Figure 1.) With right sides together, join the facings to the outside of the garment. Trim or clip the curves; turn facing to the inside. Then slip-stitch the facing to the garment.

Another way of facing an edge is to use the facing on the outside of the jacket instead of the inside. (Figure 2.) The facing itself is made by

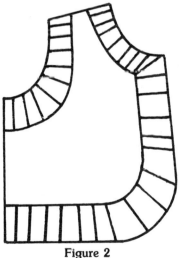

Figure 2

strip piecing to produce a rich pattern of textures and prints as illustrated by the facing in the Green Silk Jacket, page 50.

● *Knife-edged Finish*

If your garment is to be lined, you can give it a knife-edged finish by using the method described under Linings, page 3. This knife-edged finish is complete as is, but other decorative touches can be added. Cording, or piping, for example, might be slipped into the seam; laces, pleated edgings, or ribbons can also be inserted. To insert these decorative finishes into a knife edge, check the placement of your trim; baste trim in place and turn garment right side out to be sure you have positioned your decorative pieces properly.

SEAM FINISHES

When a designer lavishes hours on the decorative piecing and quilting of a garment, it is only fitting that the seam finishes be given similar care and attention, particularly if the garment is to be reversible. The appearance of every garment is improved when seams are neat, but in quilted clothing, this finishing is doubly important because it is essential to prevent batting from easing out of the raw seams.

Quilted garments require so much careful planning and sewing time that most designers consider them to be wearable art. As such they are carefully crafted, and that attention to detail also applies to seam finishes.

The inside seams of a quilted garment may be finished in any of the following ways. The seams can also become a decorative element on the outside of the garment as shown in the Rainbow Jacket, page 116. Your choice will depend upon whether or not your work is to be reversible, how flat you want the seams to lie, and how decorative you want the finish to be. All of the following finishes are based on the garment's having ½" seams.

● Flat Bias Binding

This is one of the most frequently used seam finishes for quilted clothing. It uses a strip of bias-cut fabric over all raw edges. You may use a single-fold bias tape, or you may prefer to cut bias strips of fabric to contrast with or to match your garment.

Cut strips from 1" to 1½" wide. (The width will depend upon the thickness of the batting or filler you have used and on the weight of your materials.) Sew one edge of the bias binding strip right along the seam line, right side of bias binding facing the backing fabric. (Figure 1.) Trim away

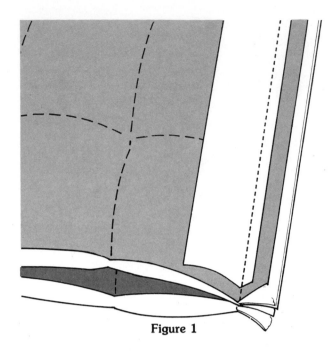

Figure 1

any excess from the garment seam if necessary. Now overlap the binding over all raw edges. Turn under the raw edge of the binding strip and stitch it down, using a whipstitch. (Figure 2.) This will cover all raw parts of the seam and will give a smooth, finished binding. A flat bias binding can also be whipstitched on both sides to cover a seam. Use a binding of a contrasting color for a decorative effect.

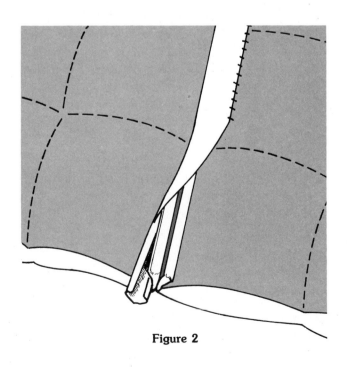

Figure 2

● Extended Bias Binding

In this finish just the seam itself is bound. A double-fold bias tape or a 2″ strip of bias binding usually works well, but you will need a wider bias for a very thick batt or a deeper seam. A narrower bias strip will be adequate for a lightweight batt or if there is just a ¼″ seam.

Trim the seam to make it even but not narrower than necessary. (One-half inch is fine.) Place the garment with right sides facing; the seams will extend to one side. Place binding strip on top of the seam line, with the right side facing the backing of garment. Sew on seam line ¼″ from the cut edge. (Figure 1.) When finished, turn under raw edge and slip-stitch the other side of the bias strip to the seam line, covering all raw edges and batting. (Figure 3.) You can sew this

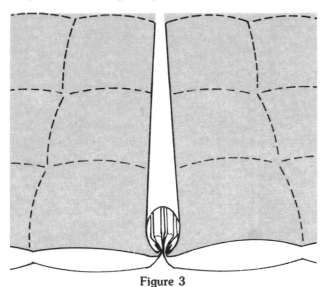

Figure 3

by machine, turning under the raw edge and making a line of topstitching on the open edge.

This seam finish can be made in a contrasting color for a decorative effect. It makes a garment reversible, but care must be taken to keep the strip consistent in width.

● Overlapped Seam Finish

For an overlapped seam finish, the quilting must stop at the seam allowance. Either do this as you quilt, or after taking seams to join the parts, remove the quilting within ½″ of the seam line on one side of each seam. Be sure your seamline stitches will secure the quilting stitches. Open up the stitched seam. Trim along all the seam allow-

ance on one side; then trim away only the outer garment fabric and filler on the other side so that the seam allowance of the backing fabric remains

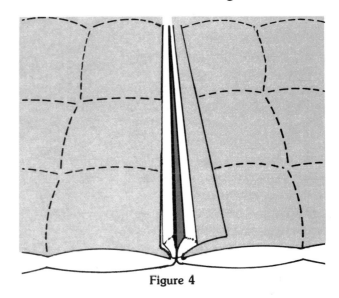

Figure 4

intact. (Figure 4.) Then overlap the remaining backing seam allowance to cover all the raw edges. (Figure 5.) Fold under the raw edge and slip-stitch into place for a smooth, finished seam.

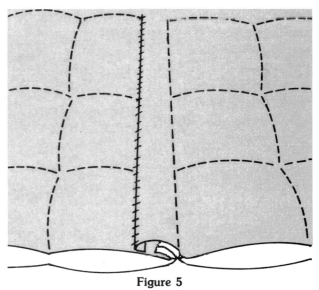

Figure 5

● Open Seam Finish

As with the Overlapped Seam Finish, this finish also requires that the quilting stitches either stop at the seam line or be pulled out to within ½″ of the raw edge. With the garment lying flat, open the seam. On both sides, trim batting and backing

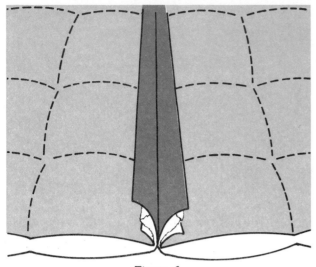

Figure 6

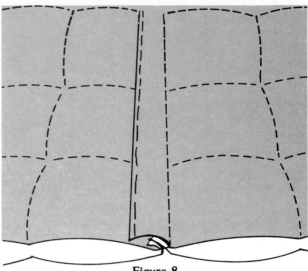

Figure 8

fabric seam allowances to within ¼″ of the seam, leaving the outer garment material extending. (Figure 6). Turn under raw edges of remaining seam allowances (this is the fabric used on the top side of the garment). Hand stitch in place. (Figure 7.) Or if it is appropriate to your design, topstitch the seam allowance in place by machine.

hand stitch a ribbon, a channel braid, or a strip of bias tape over the seam, covering from the stitched seam across and over the raw edges. (Figure 9.) The braid or ribbon can add a decorative accent to the garment. It can be used on the outside as well as the inside. It can be used to make a garment reversible.

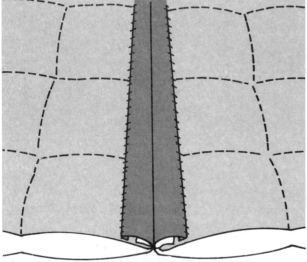

Figure 7

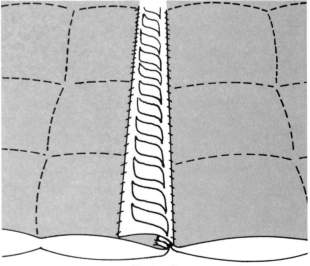

Figure 9

● *Covered Seam Finish*

This is a good all-purpose finish. It remains flat, is very secure, and is one of the most attractive of all the finishes. Trim all batting and seam allowances except for one backing seam allowance. (Figure 4.) Fold the extending seam allowance over all raw edges and baste flat. (Figure 8.) Then

● *Quilt As You Go #1*

This seam finish is for joining garment sections that have already been quilted. The quilting stitches must stop before the seam line. With right sides together, machine stitch only the outside or top fabric of the garment along the seam line.

Trim the batting so that raw edges of the

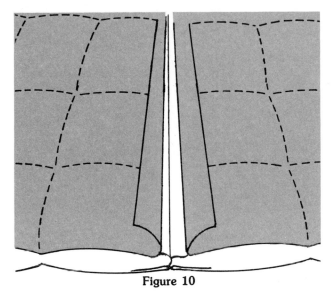

Figure 10

batting butt together evenly. (Figure 10.) Smooth one backing seam allowance over the butt joint and overlap the second backing seam allowance over that. Turn raw edge under and whipstitch in place. (Figure 11.)

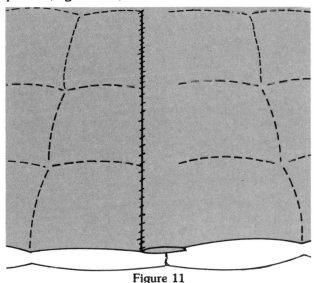

Figure 11

● *Quilt As You Go #2*

This seam finish provides an excellent finished edge for setting in a zipper or adding ties, hooks, button loops, etc. This may be used as a finishing edge on cuffs, necklines, or other edges.

It may also be used just for selected parts of the garment; for setting in sleeves, other seams will be more durable.

This is a seam finish in which the sections of a garment are quilted individually; the sections are

then whipstitched together to make the garment. All quilting must stop 1″ from each seam line. Trim the batting back to seam line. Then turn under both outer garment fabric and backing fabric so that folded edges meet. Whipstitch the folded edges together; finish quilting across the seam.

When all parts have been finished in this way, pieces can be whipstitched together. (Figure 12.)

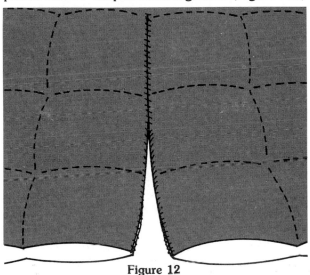

Figure 12

● *Whipstitched Seam Finish*

Place garment with backing side up and seam open. Trim batting and garment top fabric to ¼″. Then fold the raw edge of each of the backing seam allowances in, so that folded edges touch. Whipstitch folded edges together. (Figure 13.)

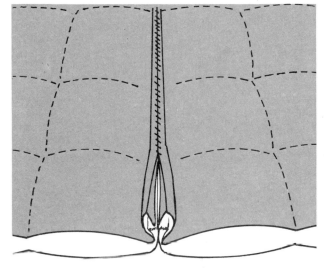

Figure 13

Decorating Garments

Appliqué, piecing, Seminole patchwork, strip piecing, embroidery, and trapunto can all be incorporated into quilted clothing. Old or new quilt blocks and medallions can be added or set in. Ribbons, tapes, and edgings also add interesting details to a design. Finally, the closures, along with tassels, ties, and buttons, give an additional fillip to the finished piece. Each of these decorative techniques is briefly described to help you select an appropriate method for enhancing your garment. For some of these, you must first transfer your design from paper to fabric.

PATTERNS ON GRIDS

Some of our patterns in this book are given full scale, as indicated, and can be used directly. Other patterns are given on grids for easy enlargement. Use 1″ grid pattern paper, or draw out a grid on a large sheet of paper. Make sure that vertical and horizontal lines are at right angles, one inch apart. Then copy the pattern, one square at a time, onto your larger pattern. Each small square on your grid pattern will equal one square inch of your pattern paper.

TRANSFERRING DESIGNS

There is an entire array of marking devices available to mark your fabric as you transfer your appliqué design, draw a geometric quilt pattern, or sketch a few lines for trapunto.

Hard lead pencils can be used to mark outside edges of appliqué pieces if you cut on the pencil line or just inside it. This way, the line will be underneath when the edge is turned under or covered by satin stitch in machine appliqué. If guide lines are drawn on the back of a fabric, the lead is less likely to cause a problem.

White charcoal pencils are available for marking medium or dark fabrics. The charcoal lines tend to rub off, an advantage when you have finished your work, but mark only what you can cut and sew or embroider at one time.

Erasable pens are still relatively new on the market. The lines they make supposedly disappear when sponged or when wiped with a damp cloth or cotton swab; be sure to test for bleeding and erasability on the fabrics you intend to use.

Transfer pencils are excellent for transferring from paper to fabric in a direct and accurate way. Simply draw your design or image with the transfer pencil, turn paper with drawn side down, and heat-set the design with an iron. Read the manufacturer's instructions carefully. Remember that your design will be reversed when you turn it over to iron; to correct for this, either iron the design on the wrong side of your fabric or reverse your design.

APPLIQUÉ & EMBROIDERY

A fast, easy, and effective way to add decorative pattern and color to clothing is through appliqué, a technique whereby a smaller piece of fabric is sewn to a larger one. This can be accomplished with either hand or machine stitching.

● *Hand Appliqué*

Simple, large shapes are the easiest to hand appliqué. Since all edges will need to be turned under, smaller pieces will be harder to handle. If you are a beginner at appliqué, try to avoid tiny circles in your initial designs. Rectangles or squares are relatively easy to sew.

Once you have determined a design for your appliqué, add a ¼″ seam allowance around the entire shape. Transfer the design to your fabric and cut out the appliqué shape. Clip inside curves, being careful not to cut past the ¼″ seam allowance. Several small clips are better than one deep clip. For example, to appliqué a heart shape, clip the fabric as shown in Figure 1.

Press the ¼″ seam allowance to the wrong side of the fabric and pin the appliqué design in place on your background fabric. Appliqué can be sewn with a running stitch, a blind stitch, or a hidden whipstitch. Be sure to keep stitches close

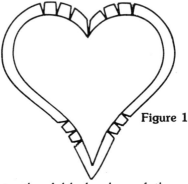

Figure 1

to the folded edge of the material. Whenever possible, overlap shapes. For example, on a mushroom, sew only three sides of the stem and let the mushroom cap overlap the top of the stem. (Figure 2.)

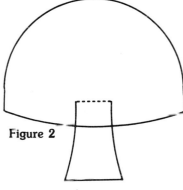

Figure 2

Some stitchers find it helpful to sew a line of straight machine stitching along the finished line of the appliqué. The hem can then be easily folded on that line. This also gives you a line of stitching to sew through when you use the blind or whipstitch.

Other stitchers find it helpful to use an iron-on bonded backing cut to the finished size of the appliqué and adhered on the reverse side of the appliqué fabric, following manufacturer's directions. Cut around the appliqué, adding ¼″ seam allowance. The bonded backing will make it easier to retain the shape as you turn under raw edges to sew.

● *Cutaway Machine Appliqué*

Trace your design onto your appliqué fabric; then cut around the design, allowing ¼″ extra. Place appliqué on background fabric; then sew a narrow zigzag stitch on top of the drawn line. Cut away the excess appliqué fabric right next to the zigzag line. If necessary, go back and sew a second line of machine satin stitch over the first

narrow zigzag stitch to catch all loose threads. This will give a smooth finish to the machine appliqué.

● *Outline Machine Appliqué*

Transfer your appliqué design onto fabric. Cut along the finished edge of the design without adding any seam allowance. Place design on background material and pin or secure with glue stick. (It will wash out later if your garment is washable.) Then sew a narrow open zigzag stitch at the cut edge of your appliqué piece. *Make sure that the outside edge of the stitch does not go beyond the cut edge of the appliqué fabric.* (Figure 3.) When the entire piece is zigzagged, go

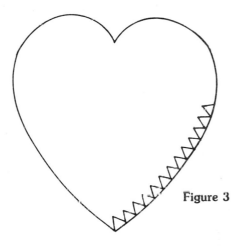

Figure 3

back and do a closed satin stitch over the zigzag line. (Figure 4.) Some stitchers prefer to use an

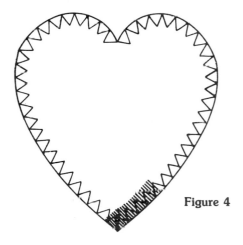

Figure 4

iron-on bonding material to give the fabric more body and make it easier to sew.

● *Embroidery*

Traditionally, embroidery is one of the most popular methods of clothing embellishment. Using yarn, floss, or silk, you can create designs that range from the lively geometric repeats of cross stitch to the completely solid stitching of Chinese embroidery. Almost any embroidery technique can be adapted to clothing. Numerous examples will be found in this book. Embroidery accents are used to enhance piecing and other decorative techniques in the child's Pinafore shown on page 125, in the Embroidered Seminole Patchwork Boots on page 144, in the Heart Pendants on page 128, in the Lacy Vest on page 43, and as a delicate inside touch for the Clutch on page 133.

PIECING

Piecing refers to any technique in which patterns are formed by sewing together small pieces of fabric. Several popular piecing methods include patchwork, strip piecing (also called string patching), and Seminole patchwork.

● *Patchwork*

Among the most popular of the traditional quiltmaking techniques is patchwork, a method of joining small fabric pieces into geometric patterns. These arrangements of the patches produce blocks or units that may be repeated. Because the individual block designs can vary in size, they work well for clothing. Sometimes a single block can be set into a bib front or the back of a shirt. A series of pieced blocks can be used on a yoke or sleeves. Or a panel of blocks might be used down the entire front of a garment.

In each case, it is important to first determine the finished size of the block needed. This is usually a function of the garment size and design. Once that finished size is determined, you can draw the design to fit.

Any traditional quilt block design can be used, but some are much more difficult to sew than others. The beginner should choose a simple block in which all the patches are made up of squares and/or triangles. If you are an experienced quilter, you will feel free to tackle a block of greater complexity.

First draw the quilt block design to the correct size. Cut the design apart into the individual pattern pieces. Pin the pattern pieces to your fabric along the straight of grain. Cut around each piece, allowing ¼″ seam allowances. Sew the pieces together to complete the quilt block design. It is best to sew the pieces together in rows. For example, to assemble the block shown in

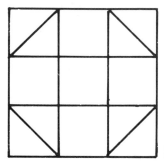

Figure 1

Figure 1, first join the triangles to make square patches for the corners by placing right sides together and aligning the diagonal edges. Pin; then sew along the seam. Press the seams open. When the triangular patches have been sewn, join the three patches in the top row. Place the patches together, right sides facing; pin and sew. Next, join the three patches of the middle row and those of the bottom row. Assemble by joining the three rows. The nine-patch block is now complete and is ready to be added to your garment piece.

There are many variations on piecing methods. Some of the books listed in our References, page 150, will suggest other ways of working and short-cut methods for piecing larger projects.

● *Strip Piecing*

Strip piecing is a simple way to join fabric pieces to a filler or backing material, and it works particularly well on clothing. Choose backing and filler materials that will give you the degree of puffiness that you want. You may use fleece, flannel, a bonded batting, or plain muslin with no filler at all. If you use a backing fabric placed with the right side down as you strip piece, your garment will be ready-lined. If you piece directly on fleece or flannel, you will want to add a lining when you finish the garment. If the garment is to be puffy and full, you must allow for the size to be drawn up by quilting; be sure to cut backing material larger than your pattern. You can always cut away excess later.

Cut the strips on the straight of grain (bias will be difficult to use). Place the first strip of fabric along one edge of your filler, right side facing up, and sew along outside edge. Place the next strip on the first so that right sides are facing, and sew. (Figure 2.) Open and press fabric with each strip,

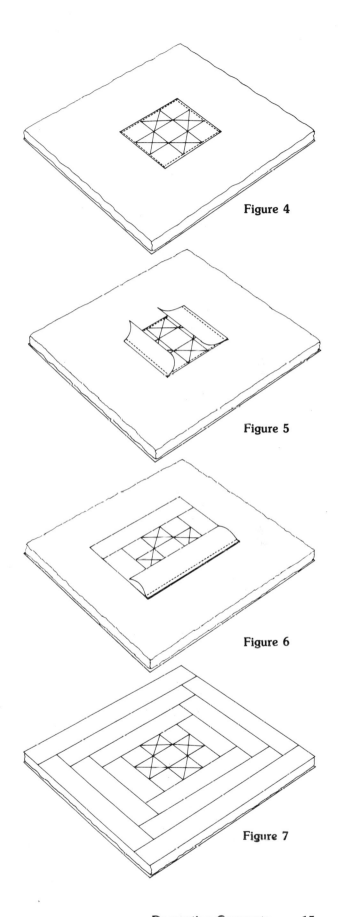

Figure 4

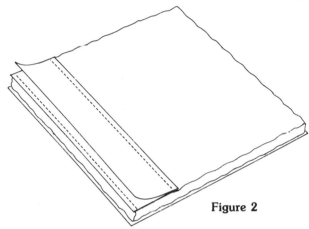

Figure 2

continuing this process until your pattern shape is covered. (Figure 3.)

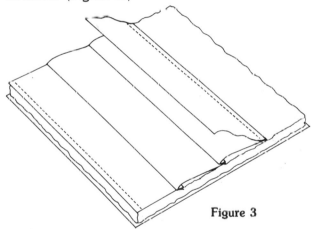

Figure 3

Figure 5

Figure 6

Strip piecing can be worked from one edge or one corner to another, or it can begin with a block at the center and be worked out. To work from the center, carefully place your center block and stitch it into place along the outer edges of the block. (Figure 4.) Stitch strips to opposite sides of the quilt block, with right sides of the fabric face down on the block. (Figure 5.) Open and press fabric, and add strips to top and bottom edges. (Figure 6.) Sew, open, press, and repeat by alternating pairs of strips until the entire area is covered. (Figure 7.)

Figure 7

A simple log cabin block can be strip pieced and easily adapted for use in garments. Any size is possible; our example shows an 8″ finished

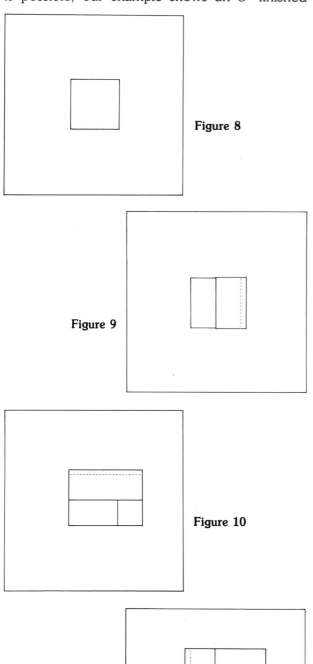

Figure 8

Figure 9

Figure 10

Figure 11

block. Cut a backing square of muslin, 9″ x 9″, allowing ½″ seam allowances. Draw pencil lines diagonally across the block from corner to corner to form a large X. This will serve as a guide in sewing. Measure to determine the exact center. Pin a 2½″ square of fabric precisely on center. (Figure 8.) Cut a strip of fabric 1½″ wide and long enough to cover one edge of the center block. Place right sides down and stitch ¼″ from edge. (Figure 9.) Press open. Cut another 1½″ strip and place it over the edge of the first two pieces. (Figure 10.) Sew and press. Continue working, adding strips in this manner until the block is covered. (Figure 11.) For variations of this block, change the shape of the block to a triangle or a hexagon.

Strip piecing is often used in garments, particularly when a quilt patch is incorporated into the design. Many clothes in this book use strip piecing that starts at one side and moves across. Strips can be of variable widths, and assorted weights of fabrics will also work well together. Strips of different widths give a garment a casual, active appearance, and strips carefully cut to an even width give a more formal effect. Strip piecing is used in the Strip-Pieced Skirt shown on page 90. Strip piecing around a quilt block is very effective on the back of a garment; the quilt block can also be set on the diagonal. (Figure 12.)

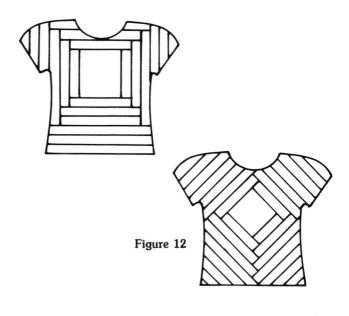

Figure 12

To use only diagonal strips on a garment, without a quilt block, mark a center line to use as a guide. Then mark lines at 45° angles. Sew strips to the garment, starting at the top and working toward the bottom. To form a chevron pattern,

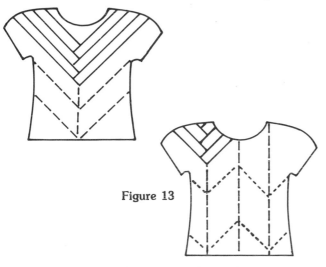

Figure 13

strip piece the sides separately and join with a seam at center. (Figure 13.) The guide lines are important to keep the angles even and the lines parallel. To use a quilt block surrounded by strip piecing on the front of a garment, center the block—either straight or on the diagonal—and

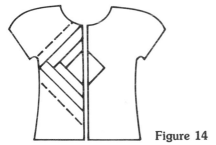

Figure 14

then add strips parallel to the edges of the block. (Figure 14.)

● *Seminole Patchwork*

This technique of piecing strips of fabric into decorative bands was developed by the Seminole Indians of Southern Florida. These intricately pieced and brightly colored bands were used to decorate skirts and capes worn by the women as well as the long shirts that were worn by men. Often these pieced bands were bordered with straight edging strips in order to "frame" the patterns. It is common to see ribbons and rickracks used in addition to the pieced bands.

Rows and rows of bands, rickrack, and plain bands of fabric are often sewn into the clothing of the Seminoles.

Contemporary artists are using similarly pieced bands to decorate articles of clothing. The number of patterns is unlimited, and each pattern is altered as different fabrics are used and as placements of the fabrics are changed. For examples of Seminole patchwork in this book, see the Seminole Patchwork Jacket shown on page 49, the Silk Wedding Dress on page 111, and the Embroidered Seminole Patchwork Boots on page 144.

The techniques for the construction of the bands are not difficult to master. You will need a variety of cotton fabrics. It is a good idea to wash and iron the fabrics before you use them, unless you are sure that the garment you are making will only be dry-cleaned. Sharp scissors will help you cut consistently on your marks. If you are a beginner, start with a simple pattern consisting of strips that are of equal width and where all of the cutting is on the straight of the fabric.

The first step in Seminole patchwork is to sew long, narrow strips of fabric into a band of varying colors and fabrics. To allow for seams, the strips of fabric should be cut ½″ wider than the finished size and about twice as long as you want the finished band to be. The number of strips and the placement of the colors depend on the effect you wish to achieve. Sew the long strips together on the machine, using a ¼″ seam allowance, and press the seams open.

Mark your fabric carefully to insure straight, consistent cuts, and cut the seamed band apart. (Figure 1.) This cut is the width of the finished

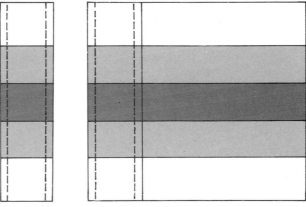

Figure 1

square plus the ¼″ seam on each side (1½″ wide for a 1″ wide strip).

Sew these second squares by offsetting them by one square, forming a diagonal. (Figure 2.) It

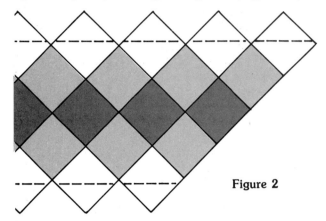

Figure 2

is helpful to first sew all strips into pairs, then sew the pairs together, and so on until the band is stitched into one piece. Press the seams open and trim the threads.

The ends of the pieced bands can be evened by removing the corner, cutting straight through the pattern. The triangular piece that is removed is stitched to the opposite end of the band. The result is a straight edge on both ends. (Figure 3.)

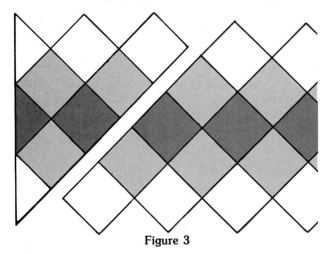

Figure 3

Patterns can be varied by cutting the strips in different widths as well as by varying the angle of the second cut. (Figures 4 and 5.) It is a good idea to stitch a sample of the band that you plan to use in the garment. In this way, you can easily make any changes in color selection or placement before you have cut and pieced an entire band.

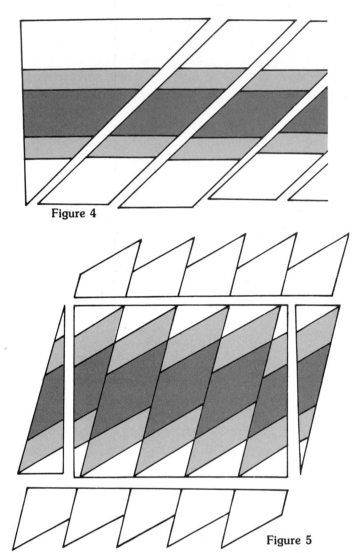

Figure 4

Figure 5

It is generally a good idea to consider adding plain strips to the edges of the Seminole patchwork. These strips act to visually frame the intricate patchwork band as well as to control the stretching on the bias edge of the band. In order to attach the border bands, first trim the patchwork. When you trim, be sure to leave the ¼″ that is the seam allowance. The cut should be ¼″ outside the points of the outer shapes. (Figure 2.)

These intricate strips of patchwork make grand additions to your clothing creations. Bands can be sewn on as appliqués or, better yet, seamed into garments. Quilting on the bands should be kept to a minimum, as it is difficult to quilt through the many seams. Quilting on the border strips can anchor the bands and add other interesting detail.

Simply pieced bands alternated with solid-colored strips all of which are set straight (with no diagonals) also make an intriguing pattern. (Figures 6 and 7.) Plaids and complex designs can be

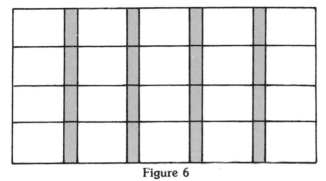

Figure 6

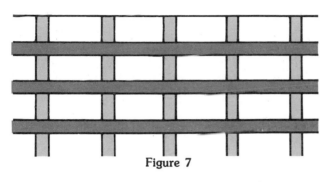

Figure 7

achieved in this way by making further color changes. See Figure 8 for a variation in which

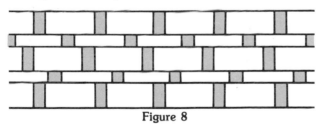

Figure 8

pieced bands are offset on one another with no solid strip.

Even random widths of fabric offer wonderful potential for pattern. The Pieced Jacket on page 55 shows the use of random widths in which diagonal and straight lines are combined.

Seminole patchwork has so many intriguing possibilities for variation that it can become a full time preoccupation. There are several excellent books available on this technique for those who are interested in pursuing it in greater detail. Two authors who have written about Seminole patch-

work have work included in this book. One is Cheryl Bradkin, author of *The Seminole Patchwork Book* and designer of the Seminole Patchwork Jacket shown on page 49. The other is Lassie Wittman, whose book is *Seminole Patchwork Patterns* and who designed the eyeglass cases on page 142.

ADAPTING A PATTERN TO PIECING

It will be simple to add a quilt block or pieced design to a garment if you have an appropriate pattern. Some garments have areas such as yokes, cuffs, insets—or any parts cut on the straight—that literally ask for some decorative embellishment. A jumper top, for example, provides a perfect spot for an insert. (Figure 1.)

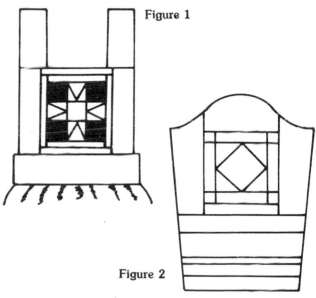

Figure 1

Figure 2

One way to determine the best placement for inserts or patchwork is to lay out the pattern parts. Choose a pieced block, an appliqué, or other embellishment for the garment, and then add to it to make a piece of fabric as large as necessary for the pattern piece. Then cut the pattern part. For example, start with a quilt block or patch. Place it on the pattern where you want it centered, on the sleeve for example. Sew bands to the sides of the pieced block, or add strips around all the edges until you have the size you need for your pattern. Then cut the sleeve from that prepared fabric. (Figure 2.)

A circular medallion can be mounted on a square and treated similarly. The medallion, when it is mounted on the square, can become the basis for the back of a garment. (Figure 3.)

Figure 3

To design your own pieced garment, make a copy of your pattern on butcher paper. Draw on the butcher paper pattern to try different piecing arrangements. When you find one that satisfies you, cut the butcher paper into those pieces. (Figures 4 and 5.) Pin the oddly shaped paper

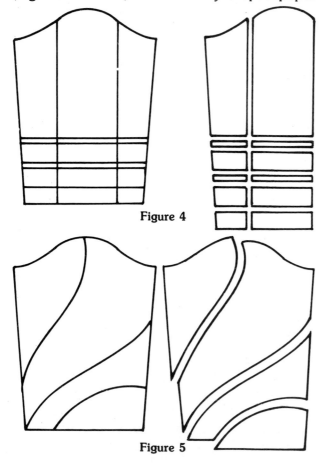

Figure 4

Figure 5

pattern pieces on top of the various fabrics you wish to piece. Cut around each pattern, allowing at least ¼″ seam allowances around each piece. Then reassemble the various pieces of fabric for one multi-patterned, multi-colored pattern piece that is ready to be assembled with others into a garment. The children's Jumpsuits, page 125, are examples of garments that are pieced in this way.

As you sew, you will begin to see other variations of these methods that you can use. For example, you may want to start piecing at the center of a muslin base for your garment section and then work out, strip piecing until the entire piece is covered. (Figure 6.) You can also cut

Figure 6

your pattern into parts and then strip piece each part. (Figure 7.) Be sure to add seam allowances

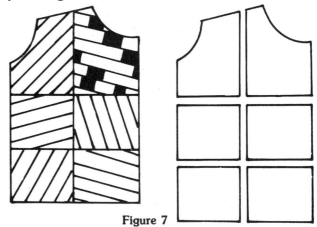

Figure 7

to each pattern part since the parts must be rejoined later. To make the sides symmetrical, place pattern pieces face down to cut the second side. Change direction of piecing within segments to mirror the segments of the first side. Many patterns and arrangements can be arrived at through variations of strip piecing. (Figure 8.)

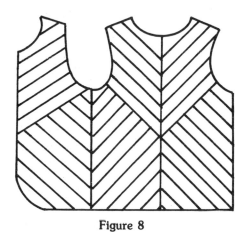

Figure 8

For books on this method of design, see References, page 150. Marjorie Puckett, whose Fan Coat appears on page 87, is the author of *String Quilts and Things,* which many of the other designers have found helpful.

TRAPUNTO

Designs made by inserting strings into stitched channels are called string padding, corded quilting, Italian quilting, or trapunto. Trapunto creates a sharply raised and dramatic design. Two layers of cloth and double rows of stitching provide channels into which are inserted cords, strings, or yarns to give the design elevation.

Begin by selecting the two layers of fabric to be worked, a front and a back. A loosely woven fabric at the back facilitates insertion of the cord. No other padding is used. Attach the layers to each other by tacking or pinning securely. Transfer your design to the back side of the double layer with one of the marking methods discussed on page 26. Be certain to allow for double parallel lines everywhere you want to form the channels. The width of the channel is determined by the size of the cord that will be used. Thread color should be selected according to the color of the top fabric. You may hide the stitches by using a matching thread color, or you may wish to bring attention to them by using a contrasting color. Sew from the back, following the drawn pattern, making a double row of regular stitches parallel to each other. When the sewing is done from the

back, front stitches are sometimes a little less regular. If your design is such that drawn lines are not required, or if you can use removable marks of some kind, do your stitching directly on the front fabric.

When all the channels are stitched, use a blunt yarn or rug needle to insert the cotton cord or yarn. Pierce the back fabric at the end of a channel and run the needle along the channel between the fabric layers and out through the backing at the end of the channel. Never pierce the front fabric with the needle. Negotiate sharp turns by bringing the needle out through the backing, leaving a small loop of cord, and heading the needle back into the same hole and along the next portion of the channel. Take care to avoid putting tension on the cording as this could distort the design. For examples of corded trapunto, see the White Trapunto Vest shown on page 44 and the Tibetan Vest on page 73.

Another trapunto method is referred to as English trapunto or padded trapunto. In this technique, large areas of the design are outlined. For example, a bird shape might be stitched on the two layers of fabric. The back side is then opened by cutting or snipping a small opening. Loose batting is then stuffed into the enclosed shape. When the desired fullness is achieved, the opening is slip-stitched shut. The entire surface of the fabric can be stuffed, giving an allover relief pattern, with the stitches forming a linear design. An example of padded trapunto can be found in the Butterfly Vest shown on page 42.

TIES, CORDS, & BUTTONS

While zippers and the ubiquitous button and buttonhole work very well, there are other fastenings that add more charm and style to quilted clothing. Many of these can be made to match the garments they adorn, and they have the distinct advantage of being inexpensive.

● *Flat Ties*

Ties for garment closings can be readily made using scraps of matching or contrasting fabric. These flat ties should be cut on the straight of the fabric, either lengthwise or crosswise. For a ½"-wide finished tie, cut a strip of fabric 1" wide plus seam allowances. A 6"-long strip is adequate for a knotted tie; longer strips (12" to 14") will be needed for bows. Fold the strip lengthwise, right sides in, and sew along the open edge, stitching one end closed. To turn right sides out, push closed end back into the tube with a knitting needle or the eraser of a pencil. Press finished ties.

These flat ties can be made in varying widths, anywhere from ¼" wide to more than 1" wide. Try cutting crosswise on a striped fabric for a lively effect. Add wooden beads, bells, buttons, or other decorative details to the ends of the ties. Even simple knots tied in the ends of the ties add a little exclamation point of fabric.

● *Corded Ties*

Corded ties can be made by covering a length of cording with a bias-cut strip of fabric. The cording is available in fabric shops, and it comes in various diameters. Should you wish to make your own corded ties, cut a strip of bias fabric to the desired length plus 1" and fold it lengthwise with right sides together. Cut the cording twice the length of the fabric strip. Slip the cording into the folded fabric strip, aligning the cord and fabric at one end. (Make sure your fabric strip is wide enough to wrap completely around the cord and to extend for stitching.) Sew alongside the cording, being careful not to catch the cord in the stitching. Stitch cord and fabric together at the end of the fabric strip with the extra cord protruding. Trim the seam. (Figure 1.) Starting at the

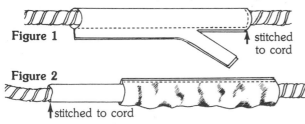

Figure 1 stitched to cord

Figure 2 ↑stitched to cord

closed end, slip the fabric back over the extra cord. (Figure 2.) It will be turning itself right side out along a different section of cord from the one you originally covered.

Once you have made the corded tie, it can be used in much the same way as a flat tie. In addition, Chinese button balls, simple loops, and frogs are all made from these bias-covered cords. Make the button first in order to determine the size of loops or frogs needed to hold them.

● *Chinese Button Balls*

This knotted version of a button offers an interesting alternative to conventional buttons. The button results from a series of knots, steps 1 through 4. (Figure 3.) The thicker the tubing, the

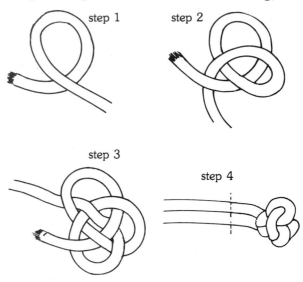

step 1   step 2

step 3   step 4

Figure 3

larger the button. Take care that the cord covering does not twist as the loops of the knot are formed. Keep the seam up and in view as you form the loops. This will be the bottom of the finished button. When the knot is complete, ease the covered cord to a uniform tightness to make a snug button ball.

Follow steps 1 through 4. The button can be inserted into a knife-edged seam (see Bindings & Edgings, page 4), or it can be topstitched to the garment.

● *Scroll Knots*

A perfect finishing touch for corded ties is the scroll knot. Just roll either a straight-cut or bias-cut corded tie from the end over itself. Tack to hold in place. (Figure 4.)

Figure 4

● *Loops and Frogs*

The simplest loop to make from a corded tie is shown in Figure 5. It can be topstitched or inserted into a seam, and it makes an excellent "buttonhole" accent on the front of a garment.

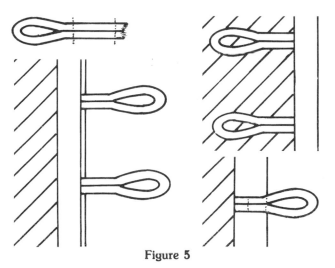

Figure 5

Frogs are extra-looped loops and are designed to be attached to the outside surface of the garment for decorative purposes as well as for function. To make a frog, follow steps 1 and 2. (Figure 6.) Secure the beginning of the loop with

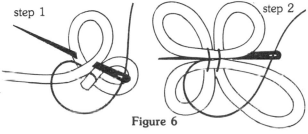

step 1 step 2

Figure 6

needle and thread as shown in the drawing. Tack down each loop as it is laid out on the garment. Leave the fourth and largest loop loose to serve as the buttonhole. Two frogs enclosing a Chinese button make a striking finish to any garment. (Figure 7.)

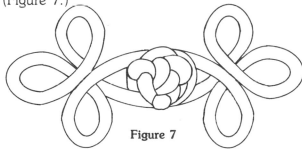

Figure 7

● **Buttons and Beads**

Decorative buttons are found on costumes from all parts of the world. It is the contrast of the hard surface of buttons to the softness of fabric that adds textural interest. Check out your sewing box (or a flea-market button collection) so that

you have an array from which to choose. Buttons placed flat on the surface of a garment can produce patterns or straight lines. Buttons and beads can be attached in decorative ways. For example, you may tie either at the ends of strings or ribbons. Do not overlook the decorative potential of the most mundane, everyday button.

● **Tassels**

Tassels come in a wide variety of shapes and textures and lend themselves particularly well to the ornamentation of quilted clothing. Tassels respond to the movement of the wearer of the garment, and they can be enhanced with bells and shiny beads. Many variations of shape, texture, size, and complexity are possible. Begin with a simple tassel from which you can create variations. For a 4″-long tassel, use a 4″-long piece of heavy cardboard or thin plywood. Wind the yarn, embroidery thread, or whatever, around the cardboard, keeping the tension uniform. (Figure 1.) More yarn makes a fatter tassel; too little

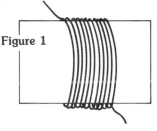

Figure 1

makes a skimpy one. When there is enough yarn on the cardboard, use a separate short length of yarn and slip it under all the yarn on one side of the card at one end. (Figure 2.) Make a tight knot

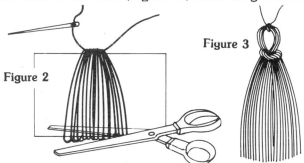

Figure 2   **Figure 3**

on the yarn where it goes over the edge of the card. Cut the wound yarn at the other end of the card. (Figure 2.) Smooth the yarn down from the tie. Using yarn of matching or contrasting color, wind a neck around the tassel near where it is tied, secure, and trim the ends. (Figure 3.)

Quilting Garments

QUILTING ON CLOTHING

Quilting increases the practicality as it enlivens the appearance of a garment. It gives a full or puffy look between the stitches while adding relief in a delicate linear pattern. Quilting also adds warmth and weight to any fabric.

The practical purpose of the quilting stitches is to hold the three layers of the fabric together, securing top, backing, and filler. Quilting further serves aesthetic purposes—adding texture, variety, detail, and pattern to an otherwise plain or flat fabric.

If unbonded batting is used as a filler, it will be important to quilt in fairly close lines to keep the batting from shifting. Lines should be no further apart than 2″ in either direction. If a bonded or glazed batt, fleece, cotton flannel, or other woven material is used, quilting lines can be as much as 6″ apart.

Quilting can emphasize or elaborate the design of a garment by paralleling lines of piecing, by outlining shapes, or by accentuating seam lines. Or quilting can produce new patterns, especially evident on plain or solid-colored fabrics. Printed fabrics tend to conceal or lose the quilting stitches. The stronger the print or pattern of the fabric, the less the stitches will show.

Quilting can be more easily accomplished while the parts of the garment are flat. This may mean quilting each garment section separately. Planning must be carefully done if quilting lines need to meet at the seam lines. On some clothes, it is possible to preassemble certain parts so that large areas can be quilted at one time. For example, a skirt could be assembled except for the waistband and zipper or other closure. The final assembly can be made after the quilting is complete. A vest could similarly be prejoined to simplify quilting. Tape patterns together at side seams, as shown in the section on Selecting & Adapting a Pattern, page 2, and cut the entire vest from one piece of fabric.

Quilting can be done either by hand or by machine. Hand quilting will leave a garment softer and more flexible. Machine quilting will be much faster.

● *Quilt Batting*

Batting (also called filler or padding) is a material that is used between the layers of fabric for quilting. It is available in either natural or synthetic fibers, by the batt or by the yard. The forms that are available will vary and will determine the "look" and function of the garment, so you will want to choose carefully. Batts come in precut sizes, such as 81″ × 96″ or 81″ × 108″. Yardage is usually 40″ or 45″ wide.

A cotton batt is not the most popular one for quilted clothes since it requires care in handling, quilting, and washing. The batt tends to pull apart, creating an uneven, thick-thin layer. It must be quilted at least every 2″ to prevent the batting from shifting during washing or cleaning. Even then, it may bunch or mat somewhat. It does give a soft, finished garment that drapes nicely. It can be used in a very thin layer and will still provide comfort, summer and winter.

Cotton in the form of sheet blankets or flannel (yardage) can also be used. Be sure to test the blankets or yardage to make sure it is easy to quilt through. It is essential to preshrink cotton flannel. A garment that contains a filler of blanket or flannel will be fairly heavy and will not be "fluffy" in appearance.

A new batt, combining 80% cotton with 20% polyester, is now available. It offers the advantages of both cotton and polyester and is bonded.

Wool is available in the form of a batt that is about 1″ thick. A one-pound batt will fill a quilt for a single bed and is adequate for most garments.

Wool yardage, called "lamb's wool," is sold in yardage shops as an interlining for coats. It is woven fabric, is light in weight, and has enough loft so that stitching patterns remain visible after quilting. The main advantage in using this wool fabric is that it is very warm but lightweight, and it does not provide a "puffy" look to the garment. Because the quilted material drapes, it clings to the body and does not give the effect of added pounds. Care must be taken in washing wool, or it must be dry cleaned. It is fairly heavy and quite warm.

Polyesters or synthetics are the most popular batts that are sold today. Their many advantages include being light in weight, warm, resilient, stable, and washable.

Bonded or glazed batts are coated with resins that permeate the web. This eliminates shifting or movement in the material, avoiding fiber migration or pilling. Unbonded batts are those that have no surface treatment at all.

Unbonded Dacron® or fiberfill in loose form is useful for padding small areas, particularly when doing trapunto-style quilting.

Bonded or glazed batting is preferable for clothing since it is coated, top and bottom, to hold the sheet together in a uniform thickness. A glazed batt that is too thick makes it difficult to take very small quilting stitches. Thickness also tends to make a garment puffy. It is possible to split a glazed or bonded batt in half so that the thickness is minimized and the garment has a softer appearance. Bonded batts act like blankets and do not require excessive quilting. They retain their loft, and garments made with them will be lightweight and warm, but they will also be thick in appearance.

Needlepunched batting is made through a process that entangles the fibers to hold them together. These batts vary in loft, with the low-loft batting offering a softer look for quilted clothes.

Thinner sheets of needlepunched batting are usually referred to as fleece and are available by the yard. Fleece tends to be easy to handle because of its sheet form. It is constructed in such a way that it is dense but thin. Fleece is suitable for a garment that you want to be thin and have warmth and washability while allowing for fine quilting stitches.

● **Quilting Thread**

Quilting thread is available in a limited range of colors, but it will be possible to find one close to your needs. How much the thread contrasts with the fabric (in terms of dark or light) will have a great effect on its appearance. A light-colored fabric can be quilted with any light-colored thread, for example. The more the thread con-

trasts with the fabric, the more the stitches themselves will show. To exaggerate your quilting stitches, use a color that is similar but darker in value. On a beige material, for instance, brown quilting thread will emphasize the importance of the stitches.

If quilting thread is not available, or if you need a color you cannot locate, use a heavy-duty thread instead. Beeswax on the thread will smooth it and make it easier to draw through your fabrics. Sometimes quilting is done with a heavier thread, a buttonhole twist, or a cord for a stronger pattern. Any strong, smooth thread can be used.

● **Quilting Needles**

The needle you use is largely a matter of personal preference. If you use a short needle, it is necessary to use a thimble to push the needle through. If you use a longer needle, it can be pulled through the fabrics rather than pushed. Traditionally, a short quilting needle is preferred.

Quilting needles come in a range of sizes from 5 to 10. The larger the number, the smaller the needle. An embroidery needle can also be used, but it is important that the needle have a thin shaft so that it can be readily drawn through the layers of fabric.

TYPES OF PATTERNS

The design made by your quilting stitches can be achieved in any of several ways. Among these designs are:

● **Seam Line Quilting**

A quilting line about ¼″ on each side of the seam will be fairly prominent on plain or solid colored fabric. Fabric that is pieced together in a random patchwork or in strips can be quilted parallel with seam lines.

● **Block Quilting**

When traditional patchwork or appliqué blocks are incorporated in the design of a garment, the quilting design can be related to the block, outlining the appliqué or paralleling the piecing. This will effectively emphasize the block design.

● **Quilting Repeat Designs**

Traditional quilting designs can be drawn onto the fabric and sewn just as they would be in a quilt. Scallops, teacup patterns, crisscross patterns, and lines can all be adapted to quilting on clothing. Templates are available for many quilting designs.

● **Section Quilting**

Quilting can be accomplished so that it is related to a portion of the garment being sewn. That is, sleeves may be quilted to suggest a cuff line at the wrist with a crisscross pattern for the bulk of the sleeve. A jacket back might be quilted to give horizontal lines on the yoke or vertical lines on the back. In each case, some lines can parallel the cut edges of the pattern parts with other areas being filled in with textured patterns.

MARKING THE PATTERN

There are many means and methods for marking the quilting pattern on fabric. Some of those used on quilts require washing afterwards, so if you are making a non-washable garment, that must be considered. Always check any marking method by attempting to remove some of it from your test fabric. Since the garment parts are almost always quilted separately, the parts are small and the least complex marking methods will work well.

● **Parallel Lines**

If you quilt lines that run parallel to your seam lines, or that outline the garment shape, you will probably need no marking at all. These can easily be "eye-balled." An occasional dot on the fabric can serve as a guide. A complete line will probably not be necessary.

● **Pattern Lines**

On striped or patterned fabric, the print itself will form a guide. Lines can follow the print, outline it, or reflect it in parallel lines.

● **Templates**

Templates are available in various designs, and these can be used to mark quilting designs directly on your fabric. Templates are often made of clear plastic to aid in marking, but you can also make your own from stiff card-weight paper or from sandpaper.

● **Needle-Marking**

Another good way to mark your quilting lines (and one that avoids all problems of removal or erasing) is to needle-mark straight lines. Place your garment (basted and ready to quilt) on a hard surface or table. Measure the areas and mark them with pencil, marking only on the seam allowance of the fabric. Lay a straight edge on the fabric where you want to mark it, and draw a sharp needle along the straight edge. If you hold the needle almost vertically, it will scratch a fine line on your fabric. Stitch on that line. A fairly large area can be marked, but not more than you can sew in one day, as the line will gradually smooth out and fade.

● **Pencils**

The use of a lead pencil is an old and standard marking method. A #2 soft lead pencil is usually recommended, though some quilters prefer HB. Lead does not always wash out and should generally be avoided on the right side of clothing. A wide range of colored markers and pencils is available through quilting and fabric shops. These are made especially for use on fabrics and work with varying degrees of success. Always test pencils on the fabric you will use.

Colored pencils are made for use on white or light fabrics. Some quilters use silver or gold pencils which show up well on dark colors. Be sure to check the pencil on your fabric to be sure it can be washed out or erased. A soft, kneadable eraser will help to remove pencil lines, but remember that pencils react in different ways on different fabrics.

● **Charcoal Pencils**

White charcoal pencils are good for marking patterned or dark fabric. The charcoal is soft and rubs off, which makes it easy to remove later. It also tends to rub off as you work on it.

● **Water-Soluble Marking Pens**

Felt-tip pens, made specifically for marking quilts, are available. The color is supposed to disappear with the use of a damp cloth or wet cotton swab. Be sure to test them on your fabric before marking your garment.

● **Carbon**

Dressmaker's carbon is sometimes used to mark patterns. It is not the best method for marking clothing as it can be hard to handle and is not easily removed. Again, check marking method with your particular fabrics.

HAND QUILTING

To hand quilt your garment, first place the backing material with the right side down on a flat surface. Then place the filler or batting on top of the backing. The backing material and batting should be just slightly larger than the top (or "right" side) of your fabric. Finally, place your top fabric or garment piece, right side up, on top.

Baste the three layers securely together by stitching a crisscross pattern over the garment piece. Start the basting lines at one side and work across, or start at the center and work out to the edges. Do not baste from the outer edges to the center, or you may have difficulty in making the center smooth. Because garment pattern pieces are fairly small (compared to an entire quilt) it will be easy to conceal knots by beginning and ending lines of quilting at the seam lines. The backing fabric, which will be the reverse side of your quilting, can be used as the lining of the garment if you conceal knots, quilt carefully, and finish the seams.

Consider bindings and seam finishes in determining how close to the edge of the garment piece you wish to quilt.

Some quilters prefer to quilt without a hoop or frame, using a table top to support the material. Others like a hoop. For clothing, either method will work easily. If you use a hoop, the process is the same as for a quilt. The quilting stitch is a simple in-and-out or running stitch. The consistency of the stitch lengths is more important than how long each stitch is, so try to develop a rhythm to keep the stitches even.

After all of the quilting is finished, place each of your paper pattern pieces over the quilted material and trim the pieces to the pattern size. Some of the extra fabric that was allowed in the beginning will have been drawn up by the quilting stitches.

MACHINE QUILTING

Quilting a garment by machine will go much faster than handwork. In planning your quilting pattern, keep in mind that machine quilting works best with patterns made of straight lines or gentle curves. A pattern that is very complex can be difficult to quilt by machine.

In machine quilting, it is especially important that all the preliminaries be taken care of before the piece is slipped under the presser foot. Carefully basting the sandwiched layers together is all important. Baste generously back and forth on the entire surface—not just along the edges. Use basting thread of a contrasting color to simplify removal.

Mark your quilting lines on each piece of your garment. If possible, assemble a test sample of top, filler, and backing. Baste the sample and try quilting it; then check your stitch length, tension, and thread color. To machine quilt, use a straight stitch that is a little longer than is usually used for plain sewing. Stitches that are too tight (too fine) will make a less flexible line than does the longer stitch. When all details are to your satisfaction, proceed with your quilting. When the layers are quilted, the top fabric sometimes moves a little. This makes the order in which you quilt the lines important. If the design is of mostly parallel lines, you can alternate directions to maintain an even look. Or all lines can start at one edge and move across to the opposite edge. Or do the quilting in the center of the piece first and work toward the outer edges. Do not start at the outer edges and move in, or you may find bulky areas and puckers when you reach the center.

When the machine quilting is finished, lay the paper pattern on the quilted piece and trim the pieces to the proper size. The quilting process can reduce the size of the quilted piece slightly.

There are excellent books available on machine quilting. See References, page 150, for some that you will find helpful.

Vests

The vest is among the most versatile of all garments. A single pattern can be used for a variety of vests when small changes are made. The evening vest is not essentially different from the warm-up vest—both can be based on a simple pattern. Embroidery and ribbons add elegance to the evening vest. Heavy batting, sturdy fabrics, and pockets add utility to the other.

BASIC VEST PATTERNS

While many vest patterns are available, there are just a few basic types of vests. A darted vest offers fit over an ample bust; a vest with a straight cut will flatter a smaller figure. Select one that gives you a good overall fit; then vary it to make an assortment of designs. Any vest pattern you choose should be adapted to allow for quilting. See Selecting & Adapting a Pattern, page 2.

Remember that you may need a pattern only as a starting point. Decide on the type of construction that will work with your plan for decorative work. Some patterns have an inset side panel; others have a single side seam. You may want to join the front sections to the back or join the shoulder seams before cutting so that all pattern parts can be quilted or decorated at one time. To do this, overlap the pattern pieces so that the seam lines match at the sides or at the shoulder. The resulting single piece of material aids in the placement of appliqué or quilting pattern. It also reduces the number of seams to be finished. (Figures 1 and 2.)

A blouse or dress pattern can be adapted as a vest pattern. Retain the curves of the neckline, shoulder and armhole; then cut the neckline and the bottom as you wish. (Figure 3.) A simple side-panel vest is shown in Figure 4. This pattern is the basis for several garments in this section. With any pattern, be sure to allow a little additional ease so that the vest can fit over a blouse.

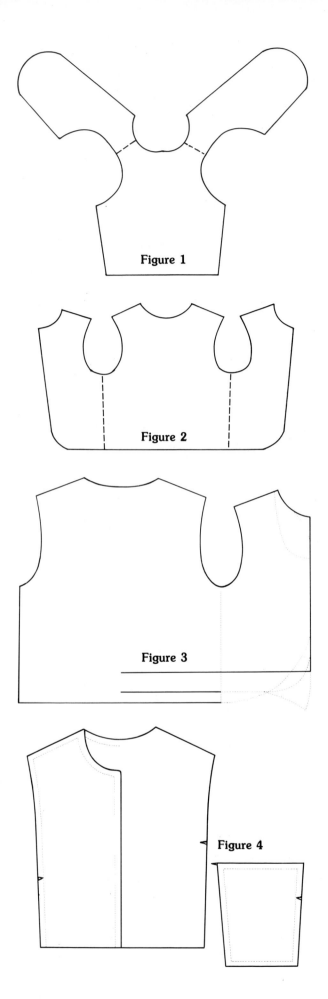

Figure 1

Figure 2

Figure 3

Figure 4

SASHIKO VEST

DESIGNED BY KIMI OTA.
Color photograph on page 31.

This long vest is a version of the traditional Japanese "Sashiko," a style of quilting involving geometric designs and used to add warmth and durability. It is used primarily on work clothes in Japan; here our designer has combined the style with appliqué in a dressy vest.

Use a simple long vest pattern or lengthen a favorite vest pattern. The style shown in the photograph is fitted and the finished length is 35". Join the vest fronts to backs at the side seams only, for both lining and outside material. Then place the lining, the filler, and the vest top together and baste.

Mark the quilting pattern, and start quilting at the bottom. Move from the geometric patterns to the stems and leaves, and on to the appliquéd iris. Only the front of the vest has iris; the back has the quilted pattern of diagonal lines only. In this vest, some of the stitches serve both as decorative embroidery and as quilting; the stems and leaves, for example, are set off with the use of green thread in the quilting. Use regular quilting in a long stitch to make the diagonal, allover pattern. When all quilting is finished, join shoulder seams. Add binding over raw edge of neck and front, and use a facing for sleeves and hem. Use flat ties as a front closure.

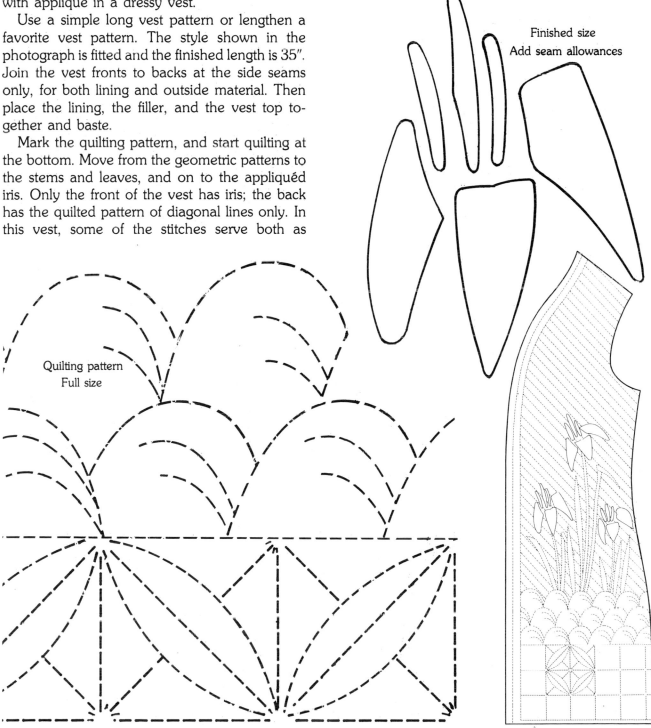

Finished size
Add seam allowances

Quilting pattern
Full size

POPPY VESTS
DESIGNED BY SHEILA COOK.
Color photograph on page 31.

Elegant poppies are precisely sewn to Ultra-suede® vests. Any simple vest pattern will work. The diagram shows placement of the poppies.

Back the appliqué fabrics with super-sheer iron-on Pellon®. This adds body and prevents fraying of the fabrics when they are cut. Transfer the poppy designs given here to the fabric by placing tracing paper over the fabric and under the poppy pattern. Trace the outlines and cut pieces. Cut each poppy as a single piece of fabric; the petal shapes are suggested through the satin stitches that are sewn over the poppy.

Position poppy pieces in place on the vest and pin well or adhere with glue-stick to prevent puckering as they are sewn down. Then satin stitch the stems as shown on the drawing, using a row of narrow satin stitch touching a row of medium-width satin stitch. Then sew the same fine satin stitch over all raw edges of the appliqué to suggest petal shapes. The curly stamen may be drawn with tracing paper or with disappearing ink (water soluble pen). Sew satin stitches over these drawn lines in a contrasting color.

Tear-away paper can be used under the Ultra-suede® to keep the stitching completely flat. Tracing paper works well, or a stiff typing paper will also do. It is removed after sewing by simply tearing it away along the stitches.

When appliqués are complete, join vest parts and add a lining.

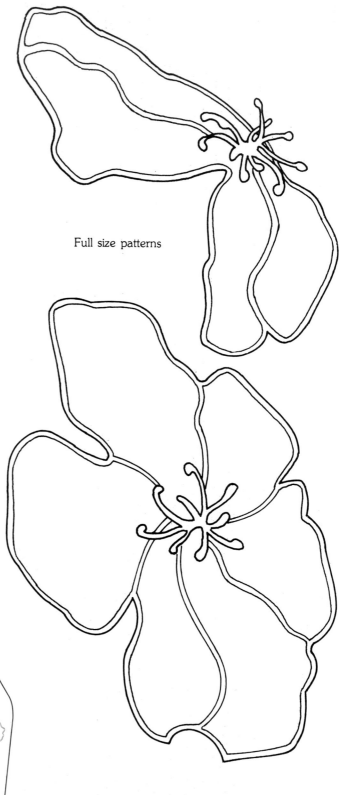

Full size patterns

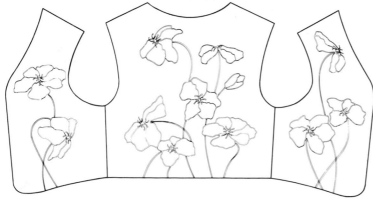

Clockwise from top: SASHIKO VEST, page 29; RAINBOW VEST, page 39; POPPY VEST, page 30; CLAM SHELL VEST, page 39; POPPY VEST; CALLIGRAPHY VEST, page 40.

Top left: LABEL VEST, *page 41.*

Bottom left: LOG CABIN TIBETAN VEST, *page 40.*

Below: RAINBOW LOG CABIN VEST, *page 41.*

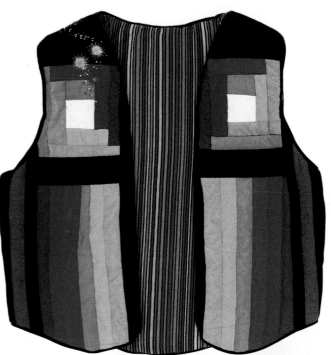

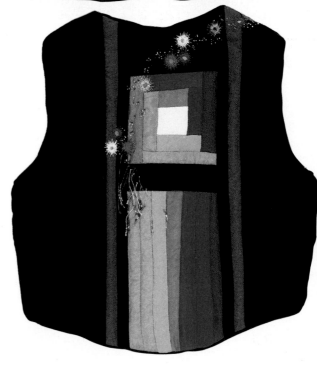

*Above, clockwise from top: BUTTERFLY VEST, page 42;
LACY VEST, page 43; EVENING VEST, page 43.*

Right: FLOWERED STAR VEST, page 44.

SCROLL VEST

DESIGNED BY DONNA A. PRICHARD.
Color photograph on page 34.

Strip piecing contrasts silk and pongee with velveteen and brocade in vertical rows on this soft and subtly colored vest. The lower 5″ of the vest is made from a tiny print; then a scroll-like Ultra-suede® design, given here, is appliquéd over the line where the print and the strip piecing join. A finely patterned brocade is used for welting or piping that is set into all outside seams and is repeated for ties. The corded ties are added as a decorative detail and each ends in a scroll-like rolling of the ties. The metal medallion on the front of the vest is an antique silver scroll to which the ties are knotted.

Clockwise from top left:
SUNFLOWER QUILT VEST, page 38; TULIP VEST, page 38;
WHITE TRAPUNTO VEST, page 44;
SCROLL VEST, page 35; UP-WITH-WOMEN VEST, page 36.

Center back

Each square equals 1″

Add seam allowances

UP-WITH-WOMEN VEST

DESIGNED BY CINDY HICKOK.

Color photograph on page 34.

Wry humor is machine stitched onto this vest that the designer describes as her contribution to the women's movement. She has shared drawings of her marvelous women with us.

This creamy vest is made from a pattern with side panels. The side seams are joined and the shoulder seams left open so that the quilting can proceed on a flat surface. Polyester quilt batting is used as filler and a lightweight fabric as backing. Drawings are made on tissue paper first, then moved around to determine placement. Drawings are then transferred by pencil (use a hard lead) to the vest. A straight machine stitch is used for the main parts of the figures, but for the hair and feet (or other decorative details) the designer changed her machine by lowering the feed dogs and raising the presser foot, allowing a "freehand" kind of drawing. The light brown thread against the cream fabric emphasizes her delightful designs.

When all the figures were machine quilted, she joined shoulder and side seams and added a lining and binding.

SUNFLOWER QUILT VEST

DESIGNED BY JUDY L. FOSTER.
Color photograph on page 34.

A worn antique quilt, in the Sunflower pattern, provides the material for this simple vest. All raw edges are covered with a bias binding of blue denim. Inside seams are finished with wide bias tape. This use of an antique quilt can be adapted to a number of styles of vest patterns.

TULIP VEST

DESIGNED BY CHRIS WOLF EDMONDS.
Color photograph on page 34.

Polka dots and prints combine with appliqué in this quilted vest. The motif is reminiscent of Pennsylvania Dutch folk art. Chris Edmonds designed the tulips that grow sturdily from their fabric stems. Using a pattern with a deep yoke and a cowl collar as a starting point, she added narrow piping to exaggerate the lines where pattern parts join. The appliqué, given here, was then added. After the appliqué was finished, the vest was assembled and quilted with a linear pattern that echoes the tulip form.

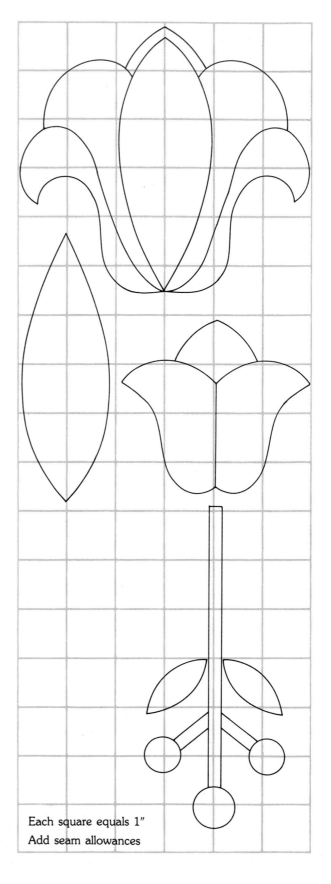

Each square equals 1″
Add seam allowances

CLAM SHELL VEST
DESIGNED BY PHYLLIS KLAPPROTH.
Color photograph on page 31.

Hand quilting in a dark thread emphasizes the diagonal direction of the quilting pattern that surrounds the appliquéd motif in this vest. A unique feature of the vest is the way the patterned pockets are set into the corners.

Choose any simple vest pattern, and cut a pocket to match the rounded front corner; the pockets of the vest shown in the photograph are 9″ wide and 10″ high. The pocket is cut from solid-colored fabric, and the 3″ circles that make up the clam shell motif are appliquéd to the pocket. Clam shells of patterned fabric are also appliquéd to the center of the back. (A placement diagram is given here.)

Quilting just outside the center motif emphasizes the shape. The quilting radiates in straight lines from the center motif. The appliqué stitches also serve as the quilting stitches, going through the batting and the backing.

Binding material used on the rest of the vest is repeated to bind the raw edges of the pockets. The binding also secures the pockets at front and bottom edges. The print used for binding is repeated in the lining and in some of the clam shell appliqués.

RAINBOW VEST
DESIGNED BY JEAN RAY LAURY.
Color photograph on page 31.

All the colors of the rainbow make this a perfect rainy-day vest. A pattern with side panels will emphasize the changing directions of the stripes. Either stripe your own fabric by seaming together solid-colored fabrics of your own choosing before cutting out the pattern parts, or use a striped fabric and then quilt on the lines of color change. The author used a needlepunch batt for filler under a seersucker fabric. The backing is a solid-colored fabric. Finish the vest, which is reversible, by adding a bias binding in purple.

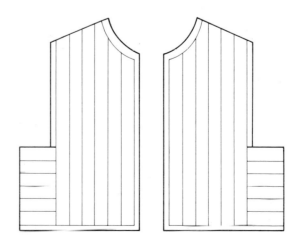

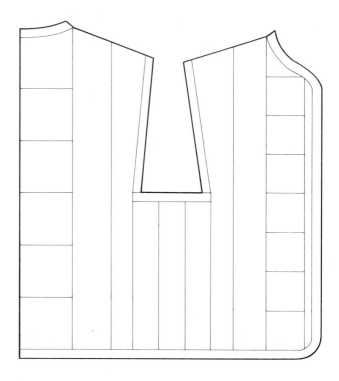

CALLIGRAPHY VEST
DESIGNED BY JODY HOUSE.
CALLIGRAPHY BY MARILYN JUDSON.
Color photograph on page 31.

This handsome vest boasts a very special lining hand decorated by a calligrapher who did her lettering with Glad Rags® markers. These are permanent fabric dye markers with a wide tip. She lettered with blue, then outlined each letter with a fine-tipped marker. Lettering of any kind is appropriate; you need not be a calligrapher. Quotations from poetry or prose in one's own handwriting add a personal touch. Children's drawings also make attractive and colorful linings.

The vest is constructed from a vest pattern with side panels. Lining is cut from white cotton fabric and joined only at the side seams. Then the lettering or drawing can be completed for the lining of the vest.

The outside of this vest is a patchwork made from striped Guatemalan fabric. Pieces are cut and rejoined to make new patterns. (See drawing of the vest assembly.) A second vest is cut from Pellon® and placed against the wrong side of the pieced vest. The outside of the vest is then assembled, sewing through the outer fabric and the

Pellon® interfacing. Parts are joined according to the pattern directions. The completed lining is then slipped inside the vest, and raw edges of all three layers are basted together. Quilting is added along all seam lines. All raw edges are bound with a bias strip of the vest fabric. The vest is reversible, giving two completely different effects.

LOG CABIN TIBETAN VEST
DESIGNED BY ESTHER HUGHES.
Color photograph on page 32.

Four log cabin blocks (page 16), in gradations of gold through rust, form the optically intriguing back for this vest. The vest is made from the Tibetan vest pattern in Yvonne Porcella's *Pieced Clothing* (see References, page 150). This vest can also be made by shortening the pattern for the Tibetan Coat that appears on page 87.

These log cabin blocks are 7″ square when finished, and each block consists of five colors plus the purple center square. The four blocks are joined to make a single larger square.

After vest parts are sewn together, all seams are covered with straight-cut binding. The log cabin section is then appliquéd onto the garment.

RAINBOW LOG CABIN VEST

DESIGNED BY BARBARA M. BOWERS.
Color photographs on back of book jacket and on page 32.

Black moiré and bright silks are the basis of this dazzling vest. To position the log cabin block (page 16) on the front of the vest, see the diagram below. Beneath each block, a strip of the black moiré is left unadorned. The lower portion of the front of the vest is made by strip piecing vertical rows of silk fabric in an arrangement of colors that echoes the log cabin block. A single strip of purple silk is added near the side seams.

The log cabin block is centered on the back of the vest, with companion strip piecing between bands of purple.

Offsetting the geometric log cabin is a trail of star-shaped shisha embroideries, scattered across the vest like fireworks on a summer night. French knots pick up all the brilliant hues of the log cabin, and as a delicate finale, bright threads, strung with tiny crystal beads, cascade over the back.

Black braid is set like piping into the knife-edged finish at armholes and around the vest. The lining of a striped fabric repeats the colors of the silks.

LABEL VEST

DESIGNED BY LYNNE SWARD.
Color photograph on page 32.

An unusual feature of this long vest with a straight front is the way in which the quilted labels stand off the surface, adding a wonderful texture and giving the vest a very active profile. The vest is simply made from muslin with a muslin lining. When the vest is finished, it is covered with handmade labels.

The "labels" are embroidered or printed with rubber stamps and indelible ink. Each is a parody of designer labels, reading "not ready to wear," "made by me," "first class," "shear delight," "man made," etc. Once the labels are printed, each is cut out, and the rectangle is placed face down on plain muslin. Each is machine sewn and turned right side out, through a ½" opening on the back. The labels are first pinned over the vest to determine placement, and then quilted to the vest by hand with the quilting ¼" inside each finished edge. The edges of the labels are butted together with not quite enough space for each to lie flat, crowding the labels and forcing the edges to stand out from the garment.

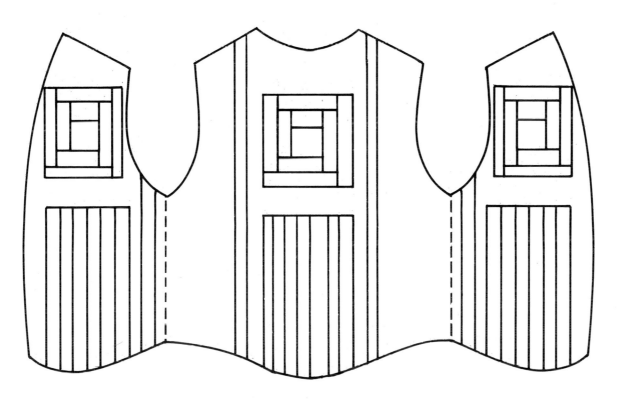

BUTTERFLY VEST

DESIGNED BY MAXINE J. WINEGARNER.
Color photograph on page 33.

A full and softly padded butterfly enhances both front and back of this lovely vest that is made of silk, lined with silk, and uses a bias of the same silk on cords and ties. Chinese ball knots (page 22) accentuate the ends of the ties. The vest is a modified tabard shape, cut 18″ long from shoulder to bottom and 17″ wide at the waist.

The butterfly quilting pattern is given here. To achieve the rounded fullness, the designer first sewed the butterfly, stitching through the silk, a layer of batting, and a thin backing fabric. Only the outline of the elegant *lepidoptera* was stitched. Then the batting was cut away outside the butterfly design. Next, this stack was placed over another layer of batting, then over the silk lining, and stitched again. Smaller details were stitched this time in addition to retracing the outline stitches. This procedure gives a double thickness to the butterfly, exaggerating the relief pattern. A bias binding of the silk fabric finishes the edges of the vest.

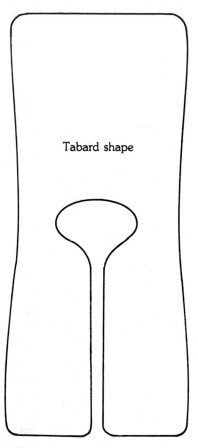

Tabard shape

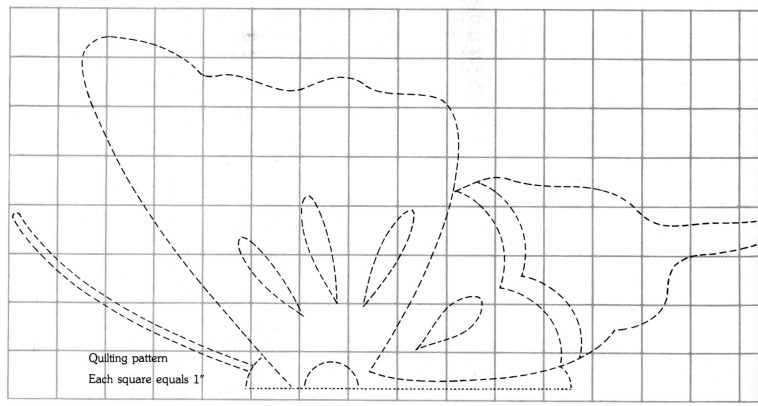

Quilting pattern
Each square equals 1″

EVENING VEST

DESIGNED BY CAROL MARTIN.
Color photograph on page 33.

A richly textured surface emerges from overlapping antique and new laces in this evening vest. Its white-on-white frosted look belies the simplicity of it construction.

The designer gave the basic pattern additional flair by cutting the edge into a free form. To cut your own free-form shape, first make a paper vest pattern. Then scallop or vary the edge, holding it up to your body to check shaping and placement. When you are satisfied with the shape of your pattern, cut the vest parts out of satin. You may want to join the side seams of the vest before adding embellishments.

To prepare the surface of the vest, place patches of velours, silks, satins, or brocades in a random arrangement. Tack these in place with a small running stitch. Now arrange remnants of lace, crochet, beading, and embroidery, so that finished edges of the laces cover raw edges of the fabric patches. Tack embellishments in place by hand. Use a single strand of white or off-white thread to match lace, sewing carefully along all finished edges.

Continue until the entire surface is covered. Add embroidery over any raw edges that remain. Then assemble the vest.

Cut a lining from satin. Join shoulder and side seams, and insert lining in the vest. Baste lining to vest at outside edges, and then bind the raw edges with machine satin stitch. Trim as necessary to remove excess threads.

The finished vest is both luxurious and elegant. Any embroidery stitches used on Victorian crazy quilts will add beautiful detailing. This technique provides a wonderful use for scraps and bits of antique lace or edgings. You may also want to try the technique on jackets and skirts, including ribbons and rhinestones as a part of your design.

Quilts often serve as reminders of the garments for which the fabrics were originally purchased. A vest that uses scraps of laces and fabrics from earlier clothes can also bring such double pleasure—the vest itself and the memories of earlier uses of the materials.

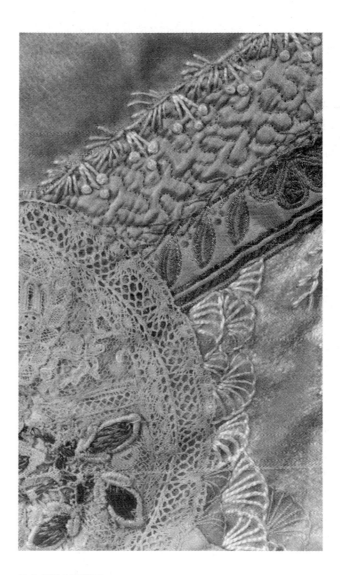

LACY VEST

DESIGNED BY RITA ZERULL.
Color photograph on page 33.

A crazy-quilt technique offers a richly encrusted surface to this vest. Using a basic straight-cut vest pattern, the designer began with a cream-colored base of satin. Off-white antique lace, new lace, ribbons, fancy fabrics, and crochet were applied in crazy-quilt additions to the vest. The designer then embellished those with embroidery of white, pink, and gold. Beads and tassels further enhance this luxurious vest; check your own jewelry box for individual embellishments from old costume jewelry. Make a lining of the satin, slip it into the vest, and finish the edges with a bias binding of the same satin.

WHITE TRAPUNTO VEST
DESIGNED BY DORIS HOOVER.
Color photograph on page 34.

A richly patterned and textured surface transforms muslin into an elegant vest. The designer used a basic vest pattern with shaped lower edges and worked her trapunto design on the separate pieces before joining them. Using a ropelike free-form design, she first machine stitched the parallel lines through the muslin and backing and then ran the cording through the stitched channels (see Trapunto, page 21). She then padded the rest of each garment piece with polyester batting and machine quilted a linear design that relates to the trapunto. The outer fabric is pulled to the inside to form a self binding (page 4). Wood buttons and fabric loops (page 22) complete the garment.

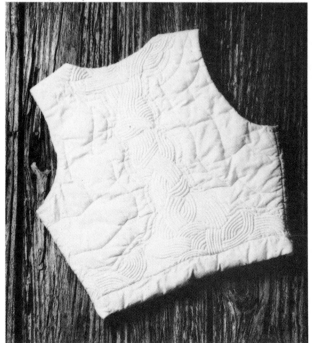

FLOWERED STAR VEST
DESIGNED BY ELEANOR STICKLE.
Color photograph on page 33.

The wonderful kaleidoscope-like pattern of this vest results from very careful and clever cutting and joining of the pieced parts. Any vest pattern can be similarly adapted by setting the pieced block into the center of the back.

The designer used a variation of the Lone Star quilt block. The block itself measures 12″ across, and it is set in at a diagonal.

By cutting the small diamonds from a border print, the designer was able to repeat the floral design within the star. Each diamond is cut with the inside point reaching into an identical area of flowers. Diamonds cut from solid-colored areas of the fabric are used to complete the design. See Figures 1 and 2 for the assembly of these diamonds into the full motif.

For instructions on setting blocks into clothing, see Adapting a Pattern to Piecing, page 19. In addition to the block in the center of the back, triangular set-in pieces complete the lower corners, and bands of fabric at the top extend the shoulder area.

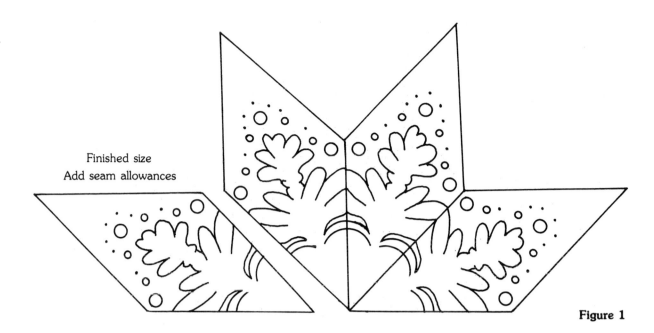

Finished size
Add seam allowances

Figure 1

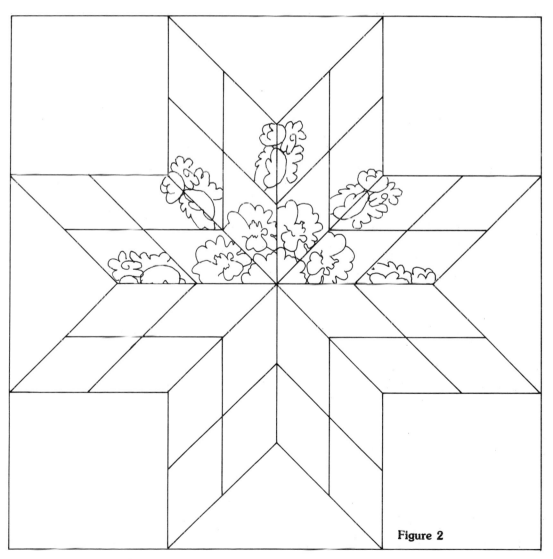

Figure 2

Jackets

Of all quilted garments, jackets are among the most popular. The versatility of this short coat makes it a part of almost every wardrobe. A jacket is worn for warmth; therefore, quilting is especially appropriate to provide warmth that may be needed for an evening out or for a brisk morning walk. The fabrics and colors will vary, but the basic patterns and construction need not.

Read the section on Selecting & Adapting a Pattern, page 2, for instruction on the additional allowances needed for the filler in a quilted garment. Then browse through this section for inspiration. You'll find jackets of silk and of velveteen, of muslin and of Dutch-wax prints, some for special occasions and some for everyday—even one made from a mattress pad.

TROPICAL JACKET
DESIGNED BY LEE MCHOSE.
Color photograph on pages 52-53.

Ordinary muslin assumes special importance when it is padded and quilted as it is in this collarless jacket made from a straight-cut pattern. A polyester batt is used under the muslin and the quilting is then machine sewn in rainbow colors. Blue and green threads are used at the base, changing to reds and oranges through the striped middle area and to yellows and yellow greens at the top. The designer completed all her quilting before the garment was assembled, and it was then lined.

This marvelous quilting design is given here. The design on the sleeves repeats the design on the lower edge of the jacket front as well as the pattern of lines. A lightening-like pattern finishes the top of each sleeve. On the back, the same lower borders are used with an overlapping drawing of palm trees.

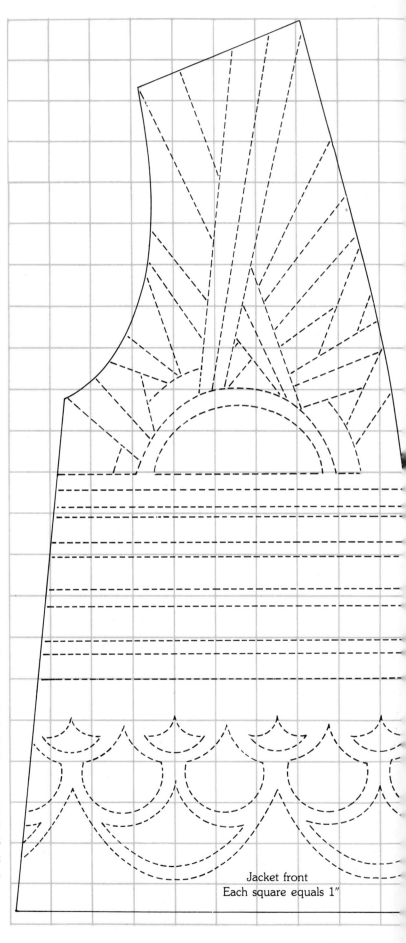

Jacket front
Each square equals 1″

Jacket back
Each square equals 1"

MATTRESS JACKET

DESIGNED BY SONYA LEE BARRINGTON.
Color photograph on pages 52-53.

The softly inviting quilted texture of this delightful jacket did not involve the designer in hours of concentrated stitching. She bypassed that part by making use of a prequilted mattress cover. Any of a number of commercial patterns could be adapted to this type of construction.

Pattern parts are cut from the prewashed mattress pad. The applique designs are then hand sewn to the jacket fronts, using a running stitch in perle cotton. The designer's appliqué pattern is given here; you might try various arrangements of the flowers and leaves. The final touch to this jacket is the rather unexpected use of a bias strip of mattress pad for binding. Because of the fullness of the pad, the binding makes a full, rounded, and luxuriously padded border.

Finished size
Add seam allowances

HEART JACKET

DESIGNED BY BARBARA M. BOWERS.
Color photograph on pages 52-53.

The sheen of red silk offers lustrous highlights to the quilting on this elegant jacket. The designer drafted her own garment pattern, but a similar style can be achieved by using basic commercial jacket patterns.

Pattern parts were cut from Thai silk, then placed over batting and lining. The quilting was accomplished by hand stitching, using white silk thread. The quilting pattern called "Heart Within a Heart," given below, is one of a collection of templates from the Great American Cover Up.®

Each part of the jacket was quilted, leaving the seamline areas open. Then, easing back both the batting and lining, seams were taken to join the jacket fronts to the back at the sides and at the shoulders. The sleeves were joined at the long underarm seams. At this point, batting was trimmed so that the ends butted together at the seams, and they were herringbone-stitched to hold them securely in place. One edge of the lining was then drawn over the other and slip stitched to make a finished seam. Sleeves were also set in this way. Finally, a bias binding was used on all raw edges.

SEMINOLE PATCHWORK JACKET

DESIGNED BY CHERYL GREIDER BRADKIN.
Color photograph on page 52.

Few piecing methods offer more complexity than Seminole patchwork, and few examples are more beautiful than this jacket. The designer used a straight-cut jacket pattern with a mandarin collar. All-cotton fabrics are used for the piecing as well as for other garment parts. One layer of cotton flannel provides padding. The jacket is set together using the strip-piecing method with the strips running vertically. Some strips are first made up in Seminole patchwork and these are then sewn in place like any of the other strips. The Seminole patchwork strips vary in width from 1½" to 2½". Our section on Decorative Considerations describes the process for Seminole patchwork so that you can make up your own designs (page 17). Strip piecing is also detailed in that section (page 14). Bias binding covers all raw edges. Wooden buttons and loops form the closure.

Quilting pattern
Full size

GREEN SILK JACKET
DESIGNED BY PATRICIA P. PORTER.
Color photograph on page 54.

A radiating pattern of colors adds a dramatic border to this jacket. Piping subtly delineates the strip piecing and the silk body.

Many jacket fronts will lend themselves to this kind of variation in which strip piecing (page 14) is used to make a striking decorative border that follows the curves of the jacket shape as shown in the diagram. The pattern itself can be cut into two parts so that the border section can be treated separately, or the facing pattern may be enlarged. Then these parts can be joined before the rest of the jacket is assembled. Sleeve bands can be assembled in the same way.

A traditional polyester batt is used as filler and the garment is machine quilted.

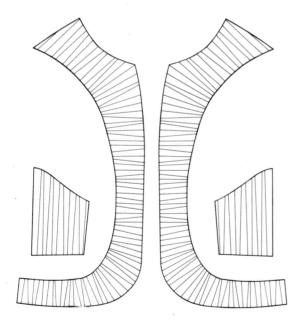

FLOWER APPLIQUÉ JACKET
DESIGNED BY CAROL MARTIN.
Color photograph on page 54.

Equally appropriate for evening wear or with pants, this elegant jacket utilizes a simple decorative method. The designer has cut a floral pattern from printed fabric and appliquéd it to the jacket in a random, casual arrangement. The jacket pattern is 31″ in length and has capped sleeves.

Join shoulder seams of outer garment fabric; then apply the print so that it scatters flowers over the shoulder seams, outlining the neck and running out to the sleeves. Next add lining and batting. (For her jacket, the designer split a polyester batt in two, separating it into two layers. This makes a thin batt but one with a fluffy surface.) Join and finish all seams, and machine quilt the entire garment in a vertical pattern. Do not quilt over the appliquéd floral prints. Finish all raw edges with a self binding.

BLUE & WHITE JACKET
DESIGNED BY MARGARET ANA.
Color photograph on page 54.

A rich array of blue and white prints adds a little restraint to the otherwise very dynamic pattern of this jacket. Strip piecing (page 14) is used as a technique for assembling a pieced fabric from which the pattern parts can be cut. Dutch-wax prints, delicate quilt-patch prints, and solid navy cotton velveteen combine to make strong dark and light contrasts.

Loops add a decorative detail to the jacket front. Here, loops (page 22) are flattened and inserted as the binding is added.

LOG CABIN JACKET
DESIGNED BY DIANA LEONE.
Color photograph on page 51.

The timeless and ubiquitous log cabin makes another entrance—this time in deep colors reminiscent of the Amish quilts. The designer used her own pattern (see References, page 150), but any straight jacket pattern with a mandarin collar can be used.

Log cabin blocks (page 16) form the front. Plain black fabric fills out the pattern parts. Sleeves are handled in the same manner. For instructions on fitting pieced blocks into pattern pieces, see page 19. The jacket is lined in a splashy print, and raw edges are bound in black.

LOG CABIN JACKET, page 50.

Above: SEMINOLE PATCHWORK JACKET, *page 49.*

Right, from left:
TROPICAL JACKET, *page 46;* MATTRESS JACKET, *page 48;*
HEART JACKET, *page 49.*

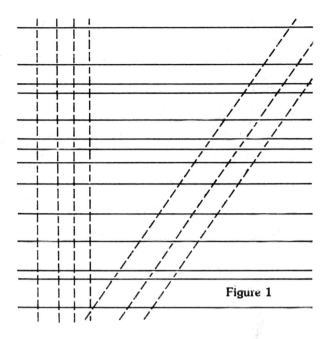

PIECED JACKET

DESIGNED BY BETTY AMADOR.
Color photograph on page 54.

A straight-cut jacket pattern with a mandarin collar was used for this jacket. The designer arranged pieced strips within the pattern parts. She first joined strips of varying widths. She then cut these into diagonal bands and straight bands. (Figure 1.) These bands were then reassembled, alternating pieced bands with solid-colored ones. (Figure 2.) Figure 3 shows the arrangement of the piecing on the jacket back. The front is done similarly but without the yoke inset.

The pattern parts were then cut from this pieced fabric. Pattern parts were stacked with batting and a printed fabric for lining. The parts were then hand quilted separately, with seam areas left open. Lines of quilting run diagonally through the solid-colored areas, picking up on the designs of the pieced parts. Each of the colored diagonal strips was also quilted next to the seam line so that the strips are given emphasis. After quilting, the jacket was assembled and the seams finished. Sleeves, neckline, and jacket bottom were all bound in printed fabric. The binding was stuffed to make a full, rounded edge (page 6).

Clockwise from top left: BLUE & WHITE JACKET, page 50;
GREEN SILK JACKET, page 50; PIECED JACKET, page 55;
FLOWER APPLIQUE JACKET, page 50;
VELVETEEN JACKET, page 56.

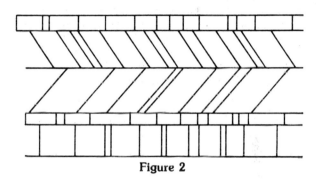

Figure 1

Figure 2

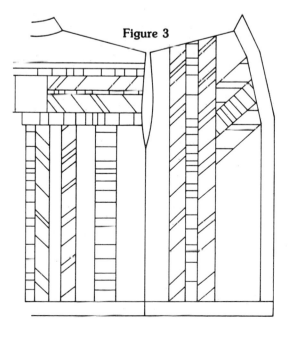

Figure 3

VELVETEEN JACKET

DESIGNED BY ELZANNA GAY.
Color photograph on page 54.

Velveteen, when it is quilted, acquires a rich sculptural surface. The soft beige jacket shown here has a filler of polyester batting and an unusual quilting design that relates to the simple lines of the jacket shape.

Washable cotton velveteen makes the jacket practical, and the quilting pattern, a series of parallel lines swirling in different directions, is indicated in the diagrams given below. The jacket is machine quilted, using a brown thread, and it is lined with a printed fabric.

An unusual detail of the design is the quilted medallion on the back; the pattern is given here. To quilt the medallion, first draw your design on tracing paper. Next, place your fleece on the wrong side of the jacket back. Center the design and pin the tracing paper to the fleece on the wrong side of the jacket back.

Thread your machine with brown buttonhole twist on the bobbin and beige regular thread on the top. Sew your design, paper side up, right through the three layers—paper, fleece, and jacket back. Tear away the paper. Pull all threads to the back to tie them off.

When the medallion is finished, change the machine to regular thread; then quilt the rest of the jacket. Quilt each part of the jacket before assembling the parts.

Finally, add a lining of a printed fabric and finish with a binding of the velveteen.

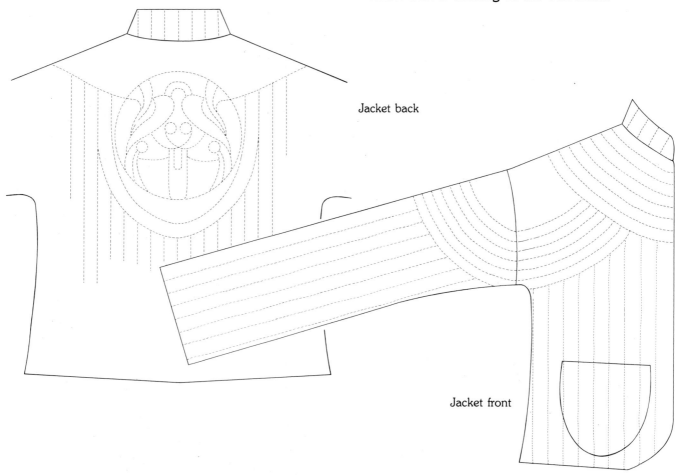

Jacket back

Jacket front

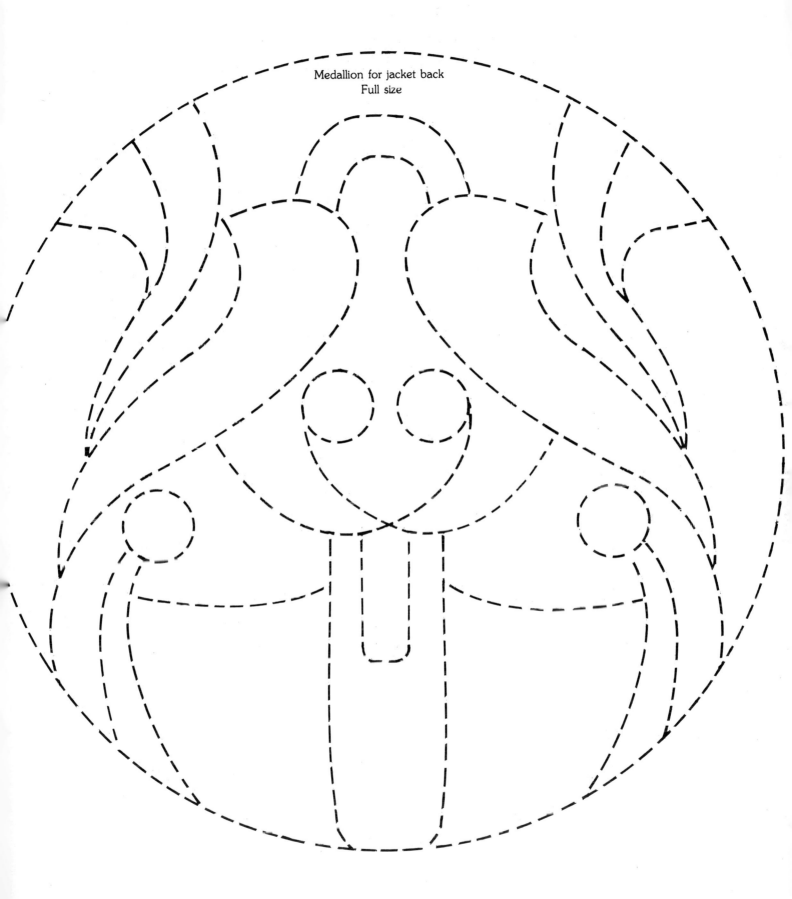

Medallion for jacket back
Full size

Kimonos & Such

Few garments have had a greater impact on quilted clothes than the kimono. This simply constructed piece of clothing makes efficient use of fabric and adapts readily to a variety of roles, serving as a robe, a coat, or as a jacket.

The soft, flowing lines and easy fit of kimonos make them popular for lounging and relaxing. We tend to associate them with the elegant brocades and silks of Japan, but they are equally at home with patchwork, piecing, and appliqué. An interesting feature of kimonos, and of most ethnic garments, is the way in which they can be folded and stored. The clothes hanger and the closet were not invented for ethnic garments!

BASIC KIMONO PATTERNS

Remember that the kimono is not a "fitted" garment; one pattern tends to fit all. It can easily be changed in size by making it narrower/wider and shorter/longer. Some traditional patterns for kimonos instruct you to vary the width of seams (from ½" to 2") to change garment size. The basic kimono shape is shown in Figure 1.

The basic kimono has an overlapping front and ties with a sash, but there are many variations possible. Each length has a different function and a different name. The hippari, which is a thigh-length kimono, is a very popular style and one for which we have included directions. It is sometimes tied at one side, although it is also worn open. (Figure 2.) The Japanese jacket (Figure 3) has no overlapping section. It is worn open. The pattern shows a thigh-length version, but it is also made in a waist-length version.

In traditional Japanese costumes, there is a curved sleeve for women and an angled cut for men. There is also a straight sleeve. The man's sleeve is closed under the arm; other versions have an open vent. All three sleeve patterns are shown in the diagrams, and they can be used interchangeably. Note, however, that the sleeves for the jacket are cut slightly shorter than those for the longer kimono. Traditionally, the kimono ties with the right side over the left.

The patterns given here are a medium size. Exact fit is not critical with a loose fitting garment, but to adjust the size of the kimono, hippari, or Japanese jacket, follow these steps:

Determine the length needed, and adjust the pattern, adding or subtracting at bottom edge.

Determine the width needed by measuring

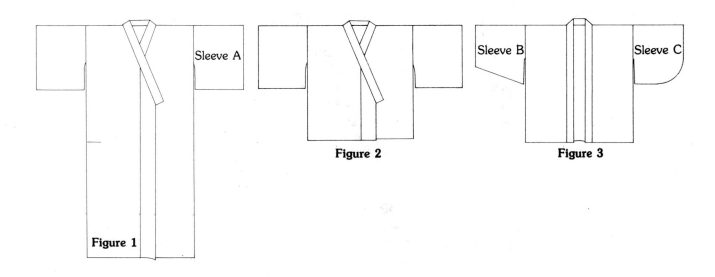

Sleeve A

Figure 1

Figure 2

Sleeve B

Sleeve C

Figure 3

from center back of neck to shoulder line, adding 4″ to that for the drop over the shoulder to the sleeve line. When the shoulder line is adjusted, this will also adjust the width of the garment. After the garment is assembled, check sleeve length before hemming.

● *Kimono Sewing Instructions*

Measure wearer to determine kimono size, and then choose a sleeve pattern. Cut kimono according to the pattern (Figure 4), adding ½″ seam allowances and making all seams ½″ deep.

With right sides together, sew the extensions along the two edges of the kimono front. Press seams open and finish seams. Turn the raw edges of the extensions to the inside and hem.

Fold the length of fabric in half crosswise to find the shoulder line. Crease to mark that line, and then measure to locate the center of the folded shoulder line. Cut an 8″ slit for the neck opening; to do this, measure 4″ on each side of the center point and cut on the shoulder line.

Fold the neckband in half lengthwise and, with right sides together, sew the two ends. Turn and press entire length of neckband. Find the center of the neckband by folding it crosswise with the two sewn ends together. Mark the center.

With right sides facing, join one edge of the neckband to the back of the neck opening. Ease neckband around neckline at shoulder fold, and sew diagonally downward until neckband crosses extension and ends at finished edge of extension. (Figure 5.) A drawn line on that diagonal will aid in sewing. Join both ends of neckband in this manner. Trim triangles from front opening and upper part of extensions.

Turn raw edge of neckband to inside, press, and hand sew the folded edge to the stitched line.

With right sides facing and shoulder folds matching, pin body and sleeves together. For sleeves A or C, join sleeve to kimono for 18″, leaving last 6″ at each end open. For sleeve B, join sleeve to kimono for entire length of seam.

With right sides together, join side seams. For sleeves A and C, join seams from hemline to a point 6″ below sleeve seam. For sleeve B, close entire seam.

Starting at the side of the kimono, join bottom edges of sleeves, sewing around the corner and

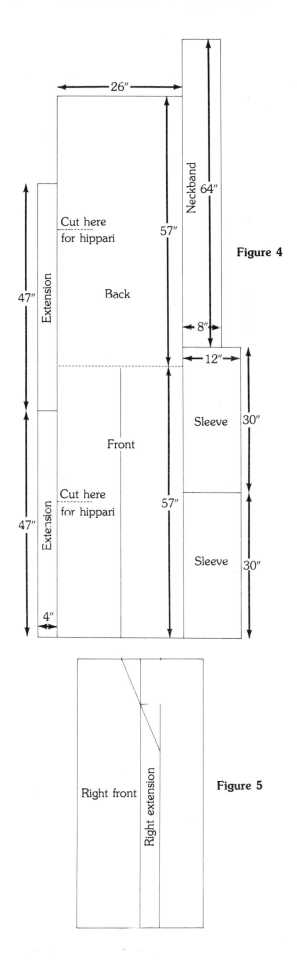

Figure 4

Figure 5

up the end of the sleeve, leaving a 7″ opening. (Figure 6.)

Hem the bottom of the kimono and the extensions. Hem under arm and all sleeve openings of kimono for sleeve versions A and C. For version B, hem end of sleeve opening.

Instead of hemming, you can bind all edges. Or lining may be used, as is the case with most of our examples. Cut all pattern parts for lining except neckband. Assemble parts. Slip inside kimono and join edges. Slip stitch lining to kimono.

To close the kimono, use a sash on the long version and a sash or ties for the short version.

To make a sash, cut a strip of cloth 5″ wide and 72″ long. Fold lengthwise and join at edges and ends, leaving a 4″ opening. Turn right side out and press. Close the opening with a slip stitch.

Shorter versions of the kimono are often tied at the waist. Make straight-cut ties by cutting strips 1″ wide by 12½″ to 14″ long and finish them according to directions in Bindings & Edgings, page 4. For both men and women, the kimono folds right over left. Left over right is used only in burial garments. The right front tie is attached to the waistline seam at the front edge. The left tie is inserted in the left waistline side seam.

● *Japanese Jacket Sewing Instructions*

Measure wearer to determine length, and then choose a sleeve pattern (page 58). Cut according to pattern (Figure 7), adding ½″ seam allowances.

Fold neckband in half lengthwise with wrong sides facing. Press; then fold crosswise to determine center. Match center of neckband to center back of neck, right sides facing. Join one edge of neckband to neck opening, easing around shoulder line and stretching down front of garment. Repeat for other side. Turn raw edge of neckband to inside, press, and then hand sew the folded edge to the stitched line.

With right sides facing and shoulder folds matching, pin body and sleeves together. For sleeves A and C, join sleeve to jacket for 18″, leaving last 6″ at each end open. For sleeve B, join entire length of seam.

With right sides together, join side seams. For sleeves A and C, join seams from hemline to a point 6″ below the sleeve seam. For sleeve B, close entire side seam.

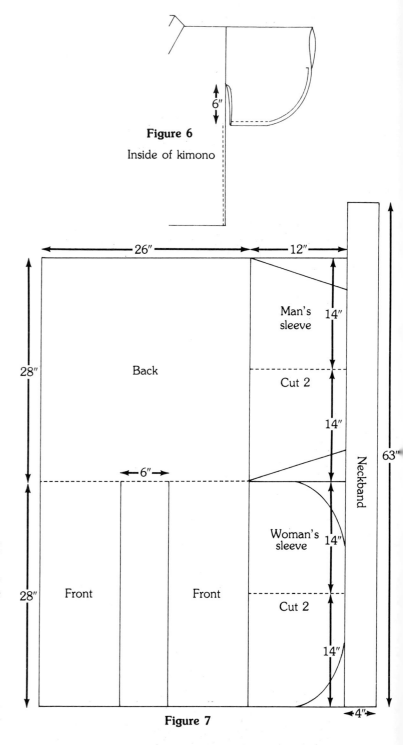

Figure 6
Inside of kimono

Figure 7

Starting at the side of the jacket, join bottom edges of sleeves, sewing around the corner and up the end of the sleeve, leaving a 7″ opening.

Hem bottom of jacket. Hem underarm and all sleeve openings for sleeves A and C. For version B, hem end of sleeve opening.

BLACK VEST

DESIGNED BY KIMI OTA.
Color photograph on pages 64-65.

The beautifully hand sewn black vest is another example of Sashi-Quilting or Sashiko, a traditional Japanese quilting method used also with the Sashiko Vest, page 29.

The designer used a simplified vest pattern, given here. The vest is lined, and the front neckline edge is bound. By using black fabric with light threads, the designer offers contrasts that allow the quilting to remain prominently decorative.

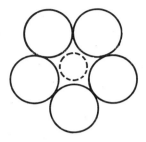

The appliquéd cherry blossoms, shown here, vary in size and each blossom is set onto an embroidered stem.

The quilting pattern consists of small rectangles, each 1″ × ½″, set together in a herringbone pattern. See References, page 150, for further information on this ancient Oriental technique of quilting.

To quilt the vest, draw quilting pattern on outer fabric. Place lining, backing, and outer fabric together, with the outer fabric marked for quilting. Quilt through all 3 layers, leaving 1″ around the edges. To assemble the vest, join finished sections. Then go back and finish the quilting across the seams.

BLUE JACKET

DESIGNED BY KIMI OTA.
Color photograph on pages 64-65.

This fully padded, quilted jacket is a short version of the pattern for our Japanese jacket (page 60).

Quilt batting is used as filler and the full, puffy effect comes through the use of quilting stitches drawn firmly over this padding. The designer quilts in her lap, using no frame and no hoop. Her quilting designs are large, graceful geometrics that are easily worked in light thread against the dark fabric.

Compare the use of the Sashiko technique here with its use in the Black Vest and in the Sashiko Vest, page 29. The geometric patterns are drawn onto the material so that large areas are left unquilted. This contrasts areas of the complex pattern to expanses of smooth areas for textural change.

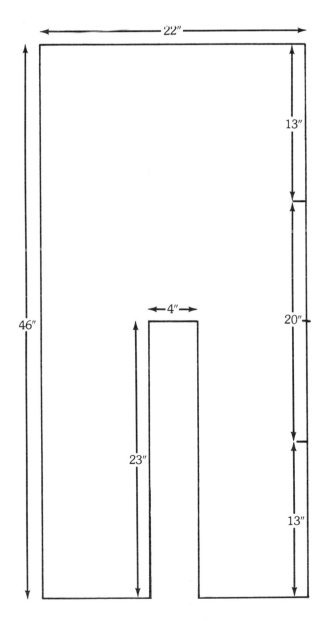

CHILD'S KIMONO

DESIGNED BY JEAN RAY LAURY.

Color photograph on page 66.

The kimono offers a marvelous robe or after-bath wrap for a child. The pattern given here fits a four or five-year-old. To enlarge the pattern, add 1″ to the body, 1″ to sleeve length, and 2″ to total length. To make a smaller size, subtract 1″ from sleeve length and 2″ from overall length, but do not reduce the width. Making up a sample garment of muslin will assure the fit, although the kimono does not require precise sizing.

The traditional Japanese method of altering the size of a child's kimono is through tucking. The kimono is made large initially. A long vertical tuck is made up each side front, over the shoulder, and down the back. This is let out as necessary.

Another tuck is taken in the sleeve. Actually, the loose fit of the garment assures that it will be wearable for a long time—probably spilled cereal and orange juice will bring about its demise more surely than growth.

This kimono is assembled in the same way as the adult's kimono with the sleeve similar to the kimono sleeve C. Follow those directions with the following exceptions.

Cut a 3½″ neck slit at the shoulder line.

Join sleeve for 13″, leaving the lower 11½″ open. Join side seams from hemline to a point 3″ below sleeve seam.

Sew up the sleeve, leaving a 5″ opening.

In our example, the outer layer of the kimono has been pieced of striped fabric to add decorative detail. The body is quilted in a crisscross pattern, and in the striped area of the garment, the quilting follows the color changes. Then the garment is assembled.

MAN'S KIMONO

DESIGNED BY BETTY AMADOR.

Color photograph on page 63.

A magnificent kimono, luxurious in detail, color and quilting, combines many of the designer's needlework skills. She used Folkwear's kimono pattern (see References, page 150), joining sections of different fabrics into bands of color for a garment that is suitable for both men and women.

The parts of the kimono are quilted before they are joined. The use of a quilting thread in a contrasting color adds vitality to the swirled pattern of the stitches.

The front band is lined and then quilted so that the stitches show on both surfaces. The sleeves are treated in the same manner. The body of the garment is lined after quilting.

MAN'S KIMONO, page 62.

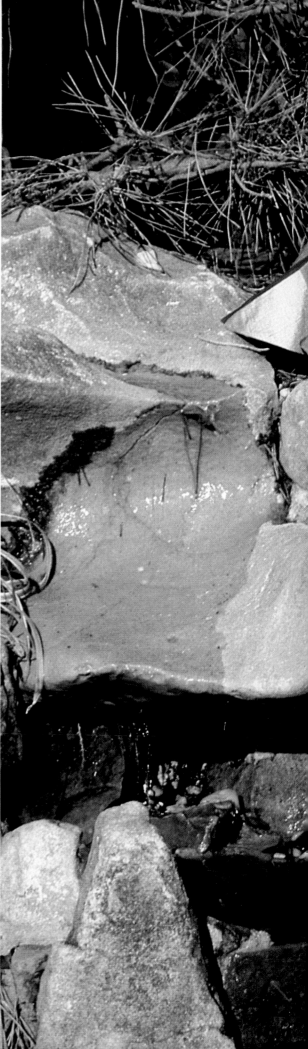

Top: *CHILD'S KIMONO, page 62.*

Right: *BLACK SILK KIMONO, page 71.*

Overleaf, from left:
BLACK VEST, page 61, and BLUE JACKET, page 61.

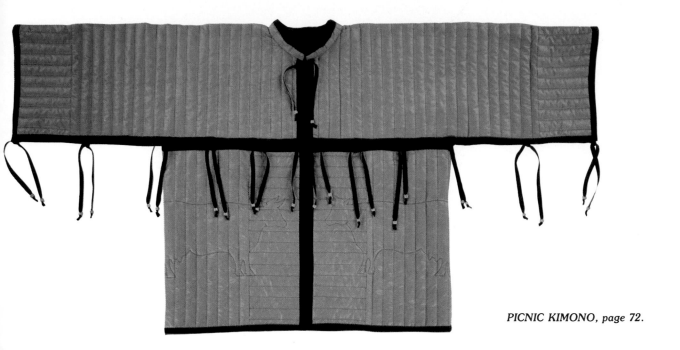

PICNIC KIMONO, page 72.

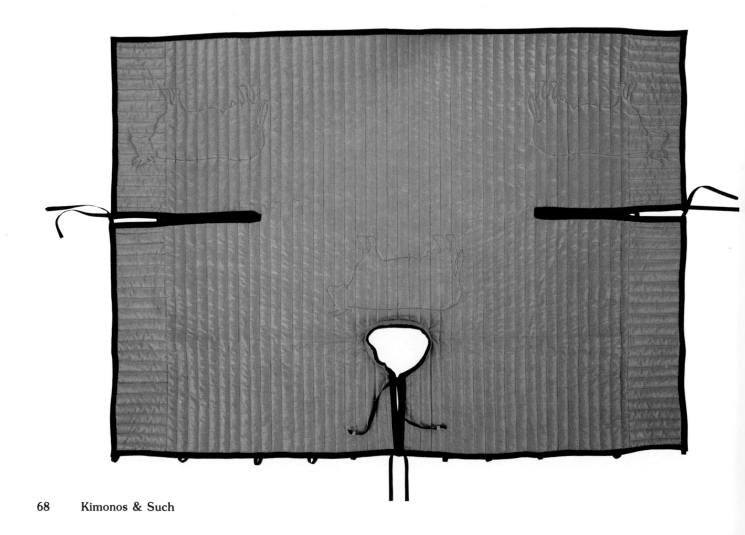

Top: TIBETAN VEST, page 73.

Bottom: CHILD'S JAPANESE JACKET, page 74.

PINK SILK KIMONO

DESIGNED BY BARBARA M. BOWERS.

Color photograph on page 70.

The marriage of Occidental patchwork and Oriental kimono is a happily successful one. Elegantly subtle colors in silk are joined around the bottom border in a traditional quilt block, shown here, and a band of this block is then combined with strips of solid-colored silk and a band of Seminole patchwork (page 17).

The kimono is made from the basic pattern given on page 58, cut to floor length. The distinctive front edge of the kimono is embellished with a four-color band of Seminole patchwork set into it. These squares measure 1½″ in their finished size. The kimono is lined in a lighter shade of pink silk.

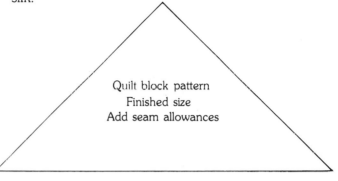

Quilt block pattern
Finished size
Add seam allowances

BLACK SILK KIMONO

DESIGNED BY SHIRLEY S. HUFFMAN.

Color photograph on pages 66-67.

This luxuriously rich short kimono, or hippari, is dramatized by sleeves edged in lustrous bright silks joined into bands. The color sections vary in width from 1½″ to 3½″ wide. The way in which the sleeve bands are faced, shown below, changes the shape of the sleeve and the directional interest in the bright silks. A narrow binding of the same brilliant colors is used to accent the front edge. A really elegant touch is the use of a 2″-wide band of the striped silks as the hem binding at the bottom edge and around the side slashes. Corded ties (page 22) are of black silk.

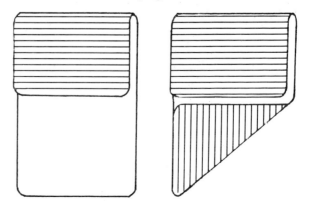

Piecing diagram

PINK SILK KIMONO, page 71.

PICNIC KIMONO

DESIGNED BY ANN DEWITT.

Color photograph on page 68.

Ann deWitt's picnic kimono or "bog blouse" is a marvel of versatility. It can be worn as a jacket to a picnic, then taken off and used as a picnic cloth, complete with visiting cows.

To construct your picnic kimono, you will need 1½ yards of 45"-wide channel-quilted fabric (pre-quilted fabric, stitched in vertical lines.) Cut 2 bands 5" wide across the width of the fabric. Sew the 5" bands to the sides of the fabric with quilting lines at right angles to the quilting lines of the larger piece of fabric. You will have a rectangle about 55" wide and 44" long. (Figure 1.) Finish seams with wide bias tape.

Fold over 11" from the top of fabric to form sleeves. Find center front by folding and then cut the neck opening, using the instructions given with the Wedding Dress, page 111. Cut a vertical line from center of neck to edge of garment.

Now, 14" from the opposite end of the rectangle, cut 14" slits on either side, as shown in the diagram; these sections will be pulled to the center front and tied. Bind all edges with wide bias tape. To make the mandarin collar, sew a 2"-wide strip of quilted fabric to the neck opening. Cut off any excess length. Finish neckline and edge of collar with bias tape. Tie the shirt with ⅜"-wide grosgrain ribbons, allowing 10" for each tie. You will need 14 sets of ties. Attach 1 set of ties at neckline, 1 set at end of front slit, 2 sets on each sleeve, and 4 sets on each side to hold front section to sleeve section. Add beads to ties.

With water soluble pencil, draw cow, given here, onto quilted fabric. Machine stitch on lines. Fold and tie. (Figure 2.)

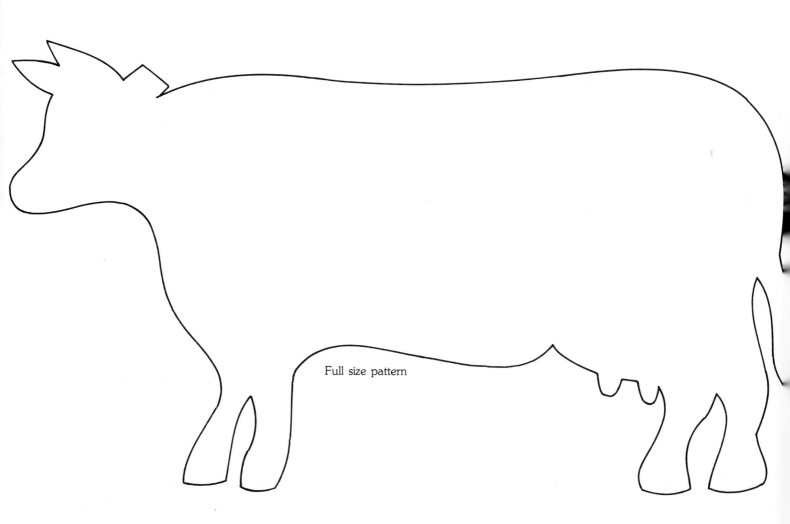

Full size pattern

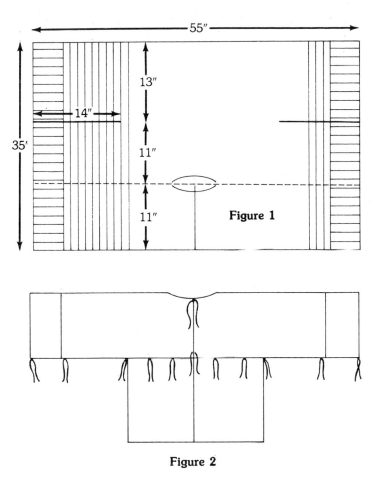

Figure 1

Figure 2

On the lower back and front are small inset panels of corded or Italian trapunto. The front trapunto panel uses a smaller design. Patterns for the trapunto designs are given here. These elegant relief patterns are set into a patchwork panel.

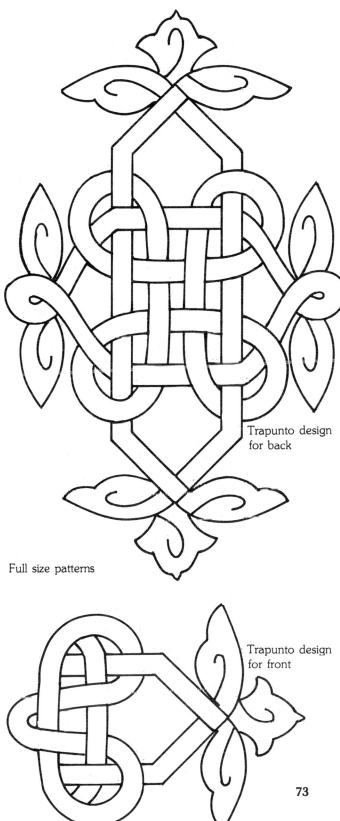

Trapunto design for back

Full size patterns

Trapunto design for front

TIBETAN VEST

DESIGNED BY JANET SHORE.
Color photograph on page 69.

An elegant vest combines patchwork, embroidery, and trapunto. The designer used the Tibetan vest pattern from Yvonne Porcella's *Pieced Clothing;* this vest can also be made from the Tibetan Coat pattern, page 87, shortening the length to 25". The designer selected rusts, grays, and blacks in both solids and prints. Printed silk offers a brilliant lining accent. Small panels of the flower print are set into the vest front. Each flower is outline-quilted and has perle cotton embroidery at the center. Gold threads outline portions of the print design.

An 8" circle of rust-colored cotton is applied to the vest back. Over it, a 7¼" circle of the floral print is sewn. Again, quilting and metallic threads offer richness and accent to the print.

73

CHILD'S JAPANESE JACKET

DESIGNED BY ANN DEWITT.
Color photograph on page 69.

Our child's jacket combines appliquéd butterflies with traditional Japanese quilting. Assorted prints are related in color to the machine appliquéd butterflies on the front. On the back, a medallion with a dragonfly picks up the colors of the prints. The jacket is reversible. Make the jacket by sizing according to directions for the child's kimono. Assemble the same way as the adult Japanese jacket. Add the appliqués of the dragonfly and butterfly given here.

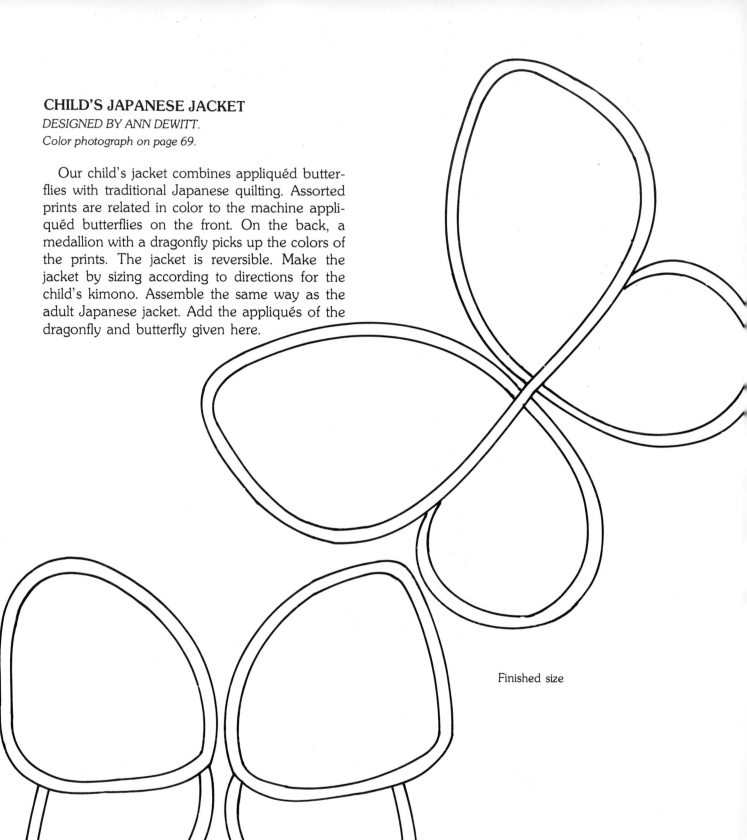

Finished size

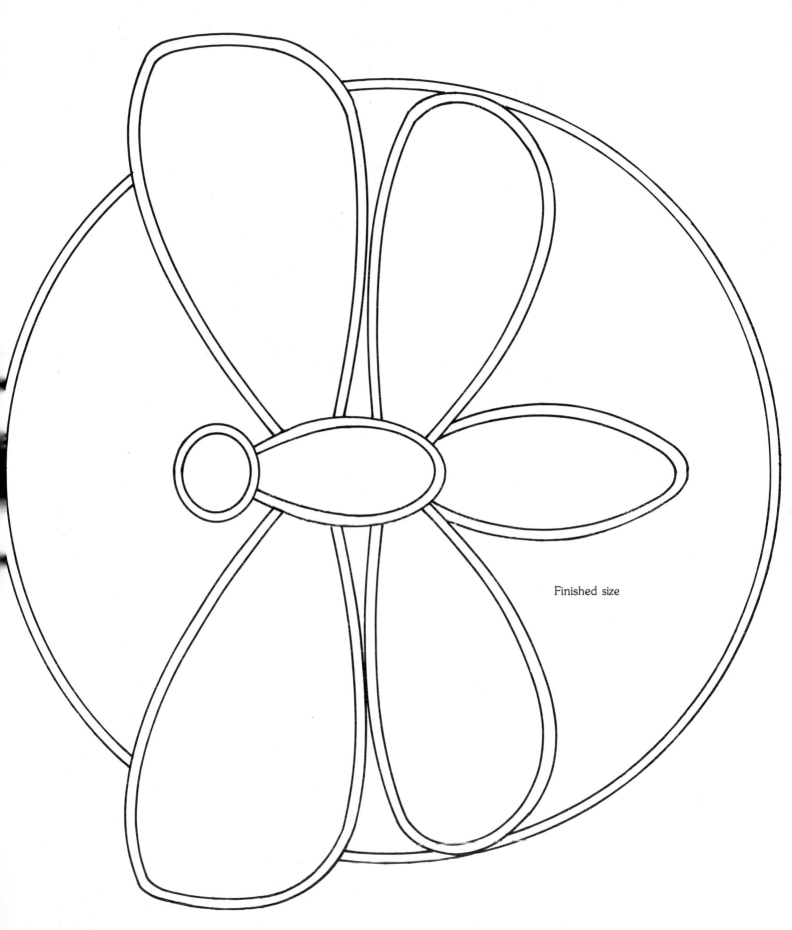

Finished size

Coats

Coats are among the most handsome garments in this book. Weight and size give them a degree of importance, but the outstanding designs are what are most impressive. Craftmanship and skill are here combined with artistry to produce wearable art, one-of-a-kind fiber works.

A source of readily available patterns that are particularly suited for quilted coats is Folkwear patterns, available in many fabric shops. To locate a source, you may write the company at the address given in References, page 150. Other commercial patterns for coats can be adapted for quilting; select a simple design, and adapt as suggested in Selecting and Adapting a Pattern, page 2. Some coats based on ethnic patterns avoid the usual demands of a set-in sleeve. And the cape, one step away from its mother, a blanket, avoids all sleeve problems entirely; the blanket is altered only enough to fit and fasten onto human shoulders.

TIBETAN PANEL COAT
DESIGNED BY JINNY BEYER.
Color photograph on page 82.

The Tibetan Panel Coat boasts a unique combination of patterned fabrics that make the coat appear more intricately pieced than it really is. A Folkwear pattern was used to create this sleeveless coat (see References, page 150), but any sleeveless coat pattern could be similarly pieced and quilted.

The designer hand sewed the piecework on the shoulder section, shown in the diagram. Major parts and panels of the garment were sewn together by machine, although all the quilting was done by hand. The coat is reversible, and the other side is an allover red print with a patterned collar and front band.

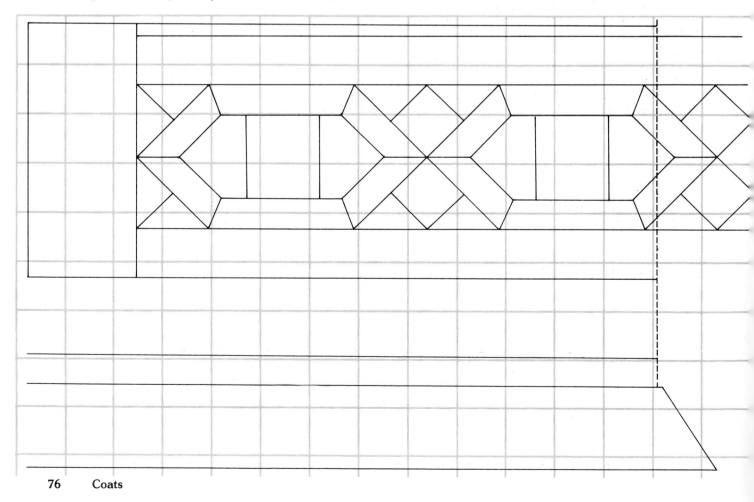

QUILTED COAT

DESIGNED BY MARLENE HEINZ.
Color photographs on pages 82 and 83.

Dark cotton and velveteen are combined with a shiny lining material in this beautiful quilted coat. A simple, dartless coat pattern was selected, and the front of the coat was machine appliquéd in prints and velveteen to suggest a yoke. To determine appliqué designs, cut a paper pattern of the upper part of the coat. Cut it into sections to achieve the desired piecing arrangement. Cut the appliqué fabrics accordingly and satin stitch by machine to the front of the coat.

The narrow lines of quilting add a luxurious body to the material along with a wonderful, linear pattern. All edges are self-bound. Inside seams are finished with ribbons of the print appliqué fabric used on the cuffs (page 10). A lightweight fiberfill is used as filler for the entire coat.

An unusual closure on this garment is made from black braid. The braid is doubled and coiled on edge so that the flat parts of the braid touch. When the desired size is achieved, the braid is stitched in place. The closure coils are stitched together, three for each side, and a loop extends from between two coils to serve as a buttonhole. The opposite side of the closure has a Chinese ball (page 22) that serves as a button.

LOG CABIN COAT

DESIGNED BY DIANA LEONE.
Color photograph on page 81.

Deep wines and burgundies enrich this log cabin coat. The drop sleeve and mandarin collar are features of the pattern from Diana Leone Designs (see References, page 150), or use any straight-cut coat pattern. The traditional log cabin block (page 16) is effectively combined with strip piecing in the manner described in Adapting a Pattern to Piecing (page 19). A printed fabric offers a decorative touch to the binding used on all raw edges. Chinese ball buttons and cording loops (page 22) add a finishing touch. Glazed fabric offers a sheen to the lining, setting off the richly active outer coat.

BLUE TURKISH COAT

DESIGNED BY WENDY BLOOM.
Color photographs on front jacket and on page 80.

Bold quilting stitches in white perle cotton enliven the gray-blue of this garment. The Folkwear Turkish Coat pattern (see References, page 150) used here is traditionally one used for men as well as women in Afghanistan and throughout Southwestern Russia, Iran, and Turkey.

Of special interest in this coat is the border quilting design which is composed of simple linear patterns in corded trapunto. The quilting stitches outline the cording. The quilting patterns for the border and the cuffs are a part of the Folkwear pattern.

A soft India-print fabric provides a colorful and compatible lining, and the inside of the border is a handwoven fabric in simple bands of color. Batting is used in the body of the coat, while the borders and cuffs have just the trapunto cording for body. The body of the coat is quilted in parallel vertical lines with variable spacing between lines; notice, however, that the pattern of the stitches (clearly seen in the photograph) is symmetrical.

BRAID TRIMMED COAT

DESIGNED BY MARLENE HEINZ.
Color photographs on pages 84 and 85.

Using the Folkwear pattern for a Turkish coat (see References, page 150), the designer made elaborate use of braid, trims, edgings, and printed fabric in this distinctive coat. One of the highlights of the garment is the elaborate quilting that shows up on the black lining like a rich textural bas-relief.

To simplify construction, you may want to assemble bands of different fabrics and braids. Then apply the bands to the fabric that forms the base of the coat, easing around curves and mitering corners

A lightweight fiberfill provides the filler, and quilting is completed on the individual parts before they are joined.

WIND OR RAIN CAPE
DESIGNED BY HOLLEY JUNKER.
Color photograph on page 79.

The handsome, reversible cape is rainproof on one side, and its reverse is a warm wool plaid. A single decorative button defines the shape of the sleeve. Any commercial cape pattern can be similarly quilted. After adapting for quilting and padding (page 2), cut cape from wool and rainproof fabrics.

Stitch the side and shoulder seams of both the wool and the rainproof sides of cape. Place light-weight quilt batting between layers. Measure and baste to mark the parallel quilting lines as shown in the diagram. Quilt by machine, beginning with the lines that define the sleeve line. When all lines are quilted, bind the edges by stitching the binding with right side down to the rainwear side, then turning and hemstitching the binding to the wool side.

Overlap front for fit. Make buttonholes 1″ and 7″ down from neck opening and 8″ up from bottom on diagonal sleeve line. Sew buttons on both sides of cape to match buttonholes.

Quilting design for cape

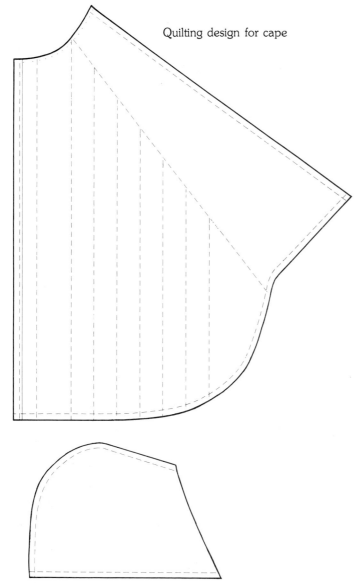

RED CHINTZ COAT
DESIGNED BY MARIE CHESLEY.
Color photograph on page 85.

The Folkwear Turkish Coat pattern is the basis for this lustrous garment of red cotton chintz (see References, page 150). The sheen of the chintz exaggerates the pattern of the machine quilting. On the outside of the coat, the accent is the pattern of tiny diamonds cut from a strip of a diamond-printed fabric. The same design is repeated in the print of the lining material and finally in the Seminole patchwork of the elaborate border. Polyester batting is used for the filler, giving a nice weight to this knee-length coat.

TURKISH COAT
DESIGNED BY MARINDA ANN BROWN.
Color photographs on front jacket and on page 85.

The elegant Turkish Coat makes perfect use of a wide border print. Made from the Folkwear Turkish Coat pattern (see References, page 150), it utilizes pattern quilting in which the quilting stitches on the borders along the hem and the sleeves outline the intricate printed details of the border. The remaining areas of the coat are hand quilted in an allover grid pattern. A quilt batting is used for the filler to give loft and body to the garment. Lined with a flaming pink polka-dot fabric, the inside is as stunning as the outside.

WIND OR RAIN CAPE, page 78.

Left: BLUE TURKISH COAT, page 77.

Below: LOG CABIN COAT, page 77.

Right: TIBETAN SLEEVELESS COAT, page 87.

Coats　81

Left: *TIBETAN PANEL COAT, page 76.*

Below: *QUILTED COAT (detail), page 77.*

Right: *QUILTED COAT, page 77.*

Right, from left:
TURKISH COAT, page 78;
BRAID TRIMMED COAT, page 77;
RED CHINTZ COAT, page 78.

Left: RED CHINTZ COAT
(detail), page 78.

Below: BRAID TRIMMED COAT
(detail), page 77.

FAN EVENING COAT

DESIGNED BY MARJORIE PUCKETT.

Color photograph on page 86.

Velveteen and satin, always elegant fabrics, are given added dimension as shades of the materials are strip pieced into borders, both inside and out, of this evening coat. Any simple jacket or coat pattern could be adapted to this embellishment in which the major decorative element is in the strip-pieced facings. A wide facing for the light side of this reversible garment is strip pieced (page 14) over quilt batting, creating a puffiness on each strip. A narrower band for the dark coat is sewn in the same way. Many "wrong" sides of fabrics were employed to give a quiet interplay of colors and patterns. Heavy batting is used in the coat, while a much lighter batt is used for the sleeves. This avoids any excess bulkiness around the arms. The luxurious combination of velveteens with satins offers contrast between the inside and the outside of the garment.

TIBETAN SLEEVELESS COAT

DESIGNED BY YVONNE PORCELLA.

Color photograph on page 81.

The rich mosaic of color in prints and patterns makes this Tibetan sleeveless coat a standout. Using a pattern from her own book (see References, page 150), Yvonne Porcella assembled row after row of intricate patchwork. She lined the coat in an entirely different range of colors and prints to make it reversible. The pattern for the Tibetan Sleeveless Coat, which can also be used for the Tibetan Vest and the Log Cabin Tibetan Vest, is reprinted here with permission.

In this long, sleeveless coat (Figure 1), narrow panels alternate with long triangular panels. A wide center panel forms an exaggerated lifted shoulder. The wide neckband folds down to form a collar and panel down the front. The coat is very loose-fitting, and one size usually fits all, but you may want to cut panels wider or narrower to

FAN EVENING COAT, page 87.

change sizes. For a garment as elaborate as a coat, it is a good idea to make up a muslin model and check for fit. If you use strip piecing, you will not need padding between top layer and lining.

Each of the pattern pieces (Figure 2) is to be used to cut the outside fabric and the lining fabric.

First plan which parts of the pattern you will strip piece. Piece fabric large enough for the strip-pieced sections; lay pattern on top of pieced fabric and cut the pattern parts.

Cut outside and lining pieces for both center back and front sections. Sew the narrow ends of the center front panels to the center back as shown, matching outside edges. (Figure 3.) Cut neck band of outer fabric and lining. Place right sides together, add interfacing, and sew along raw edge. Turn and press. Match center of neck

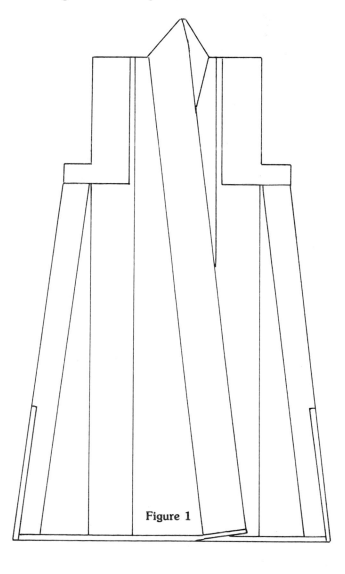

Figure 1

band with center of neck opening and sew band to neck opening, right sides together. Press seam, turn lining to inside, and whipstitch closed.

Join center panel to shoulder pieces. Sew shoulder panels to center front and back panels, starting at the front hem, going over the shoulder and ending at the back hem. (Figure 4.)

To assemble the underarm sections, first notice that each gore has a straight side and an angled side. Sew straight sides of gores to each side of the underarm side panel. (Figure 5.) Assemble lining for these garment pieces. Bind top edges of underarm side units. Starting at the hem, cut a 14″ slit from top layer and lining at the center of the underarm side panel. (Figure 5.) Sew binding

around slit. Whipstitch binding to lining.

With right sides together sew side panels to center front and back panels, sewing from the hem up. (Figure 6.) This seam will finish the armhole edge. Bind hem of coat.

Another decorative layer can be added to the shoulders so that they will stand away from the body. The shoulder panel, which was not used on this example but was used on the Log Cabin Tibetan Vest, is made of two pieces. (Figure 7.) Include seam allowances before cutting panel. Cut shoulder panel. Turn in hem edges and appliqué to the coat. Sew small piece to lower edge of panel. Pin panel to coat. Whipstitch edges to coat and around armhole. (Figure 1.)

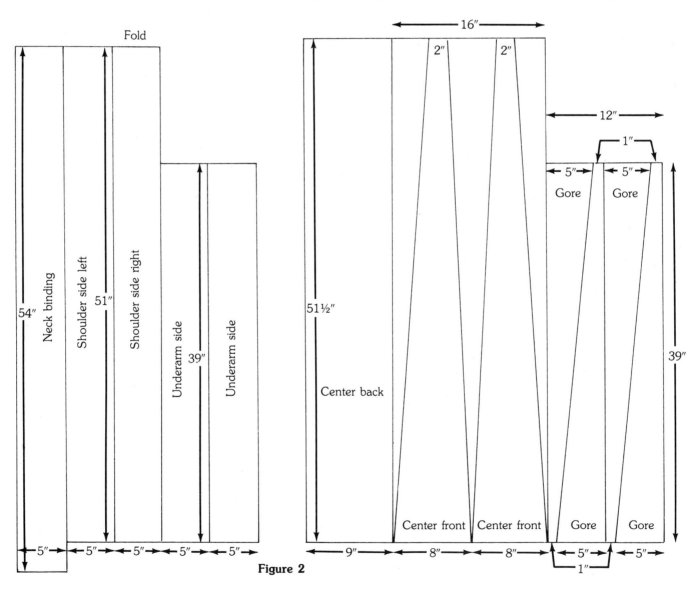

Figure 2

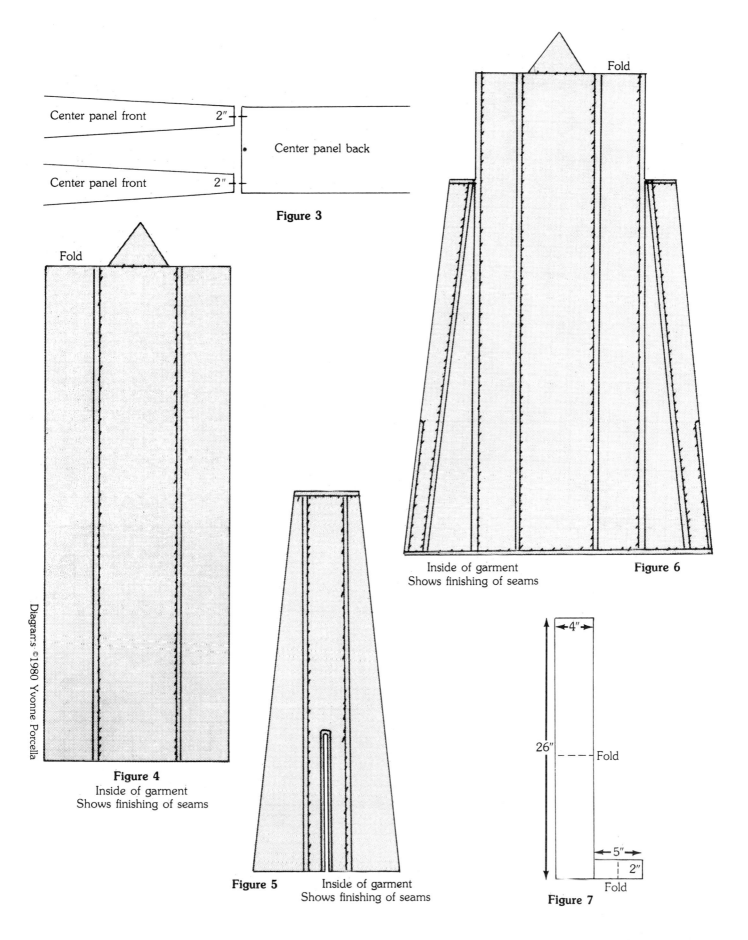

Center panel front   2″

Center panel back

Center panel front   2″

Figure 3

Fold

Figure 4
Inside of garment
Shows finishing of seams

Fold

Inside of garment
Shows finishing of seams   **Figure 6**

Figure 5   Inside of garment
Shows finishing of seams

←4″→

26″ ---Fold

←5″→
2″
Fold

Figure 7

Diagrams ©1980 Yvonne Porcella

Dresses, Skirts & Tops

Patchwork, piecing, and appliqué flourish on the garments in this section. Large expanses of material, as on skirts, allow for strong and vigorous patterns. In tops and pullovers, smaller areas of exquisite needlework set off a yoke, a bodice, or a panel. Note in this section how the garment pattern is often selected for the specific needs of the decorative work. For suggestions on setting blocks or other decorative elements into pattern pieces, see Adapting a Pattern to Piecing, page 19. A jumper pattern, for example, is easily modified by setting a block into the jumper top. Dresses are enhanced by the simple addition of a pieced block or an appliqué design.

STRIP-PIECED SKIRT

DESIGNED BY NANCY J. MARTIN.
Color photograph on pages 106-107.

Strip piecing is the technique used to make a skirt in which a sewing-basket collection of fabrics adds variety to basic color selections. Here, all printed fabrics are used in a skirt that uses mostly blues and wines in many fabrics.

Strips of fabric vary in width from 1½" to 3" wide. These strips are sewn to pattern pieces that are first cut from muslin. (See directions for Strip Piecing, page 14.)

In this wraparound skirt there are seven gores; notice that the diagonal lines of the strip piecing alternate in direction and form a pattern that is similar to a chevron as it goes around the skirt. Antique lace strips are incorporated into the strip piecing, sometimes set into the seam and allowed to ruffle out from the body of the skirt to add another dimension.

PIECED STAR PULLOVER

DESIGNED BY ELLEN EDITH.
Color photograph on pages 106-107.

Assorted prints of close value offer a complexity to the pieced star in this pullover. The designer suggests you start with any pattern that has a pieced square set into the front or back. Folkwear patterns for the Gaza dress or Egyptian shirt would work well. (See References, page 150.)

Antique Chinese embroidered ribbon is applied to the shirt front just below the neck opening. Then satin ribbons are topstitched over the ribbon selvedges. The pieced star quilt block, the pattern for which appears here, is appliquéd onto the shirt front just below the ribbons. A strip of binding is topstitched to cover the raw edges of the quilt block.

The sleeves repeat the use of the ribbons and the prints from the block design. Pieced triangles are added, echoing the piecework block, and a cuff of rich, deep, navy velveteen finishes the sleeve.

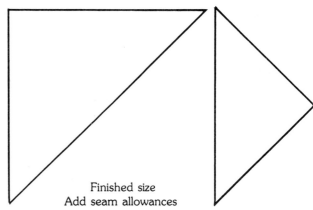

Finished size
Add seam allowances

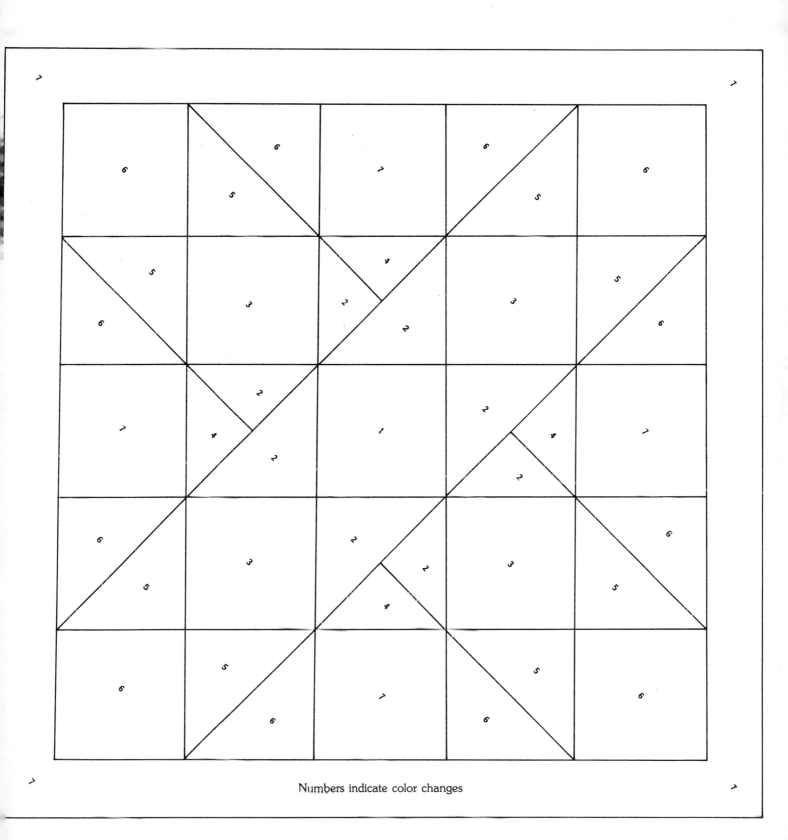

Numbers indicate color changes

PAISLEY PRINT DRESS
DESIGNED BY CINDY SUMMERFIELD.
Color photograph on pages 106-107.

A paisley print inspired the decorative work on this soft, full dress that cascades in gentle gathers from a pieced yoke. Colors within the print are used as accents for piping, for bands on skirt and sleeves, and for log cabin blocks.

The designer first made up the yoke, using a patchwork log cabin block, given here, in which the widths of the strips vary. The left and right yokes are identical but in mirror image, so the pattern must be reversed for the second side.

Piping adds a nice finishing line at the neckline and yoke seams as well as where bands are appliquéd to the skirt and sleeves. The bands, also in varying widths, are given here. Join the three bands to make one wide band. Appliqué these to the skirt and sleeve sections, inserting the piping when joining the top edge of the band to the dress part. The lower raw edge of each band is turned under and hand stitched.

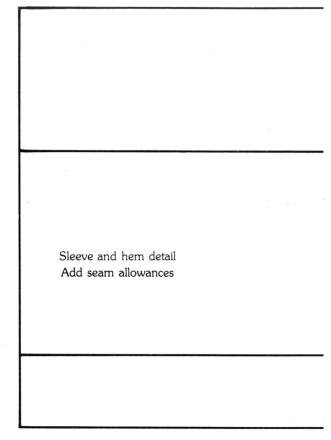

Sleeve and hem detail
Add seam allowances

Center front

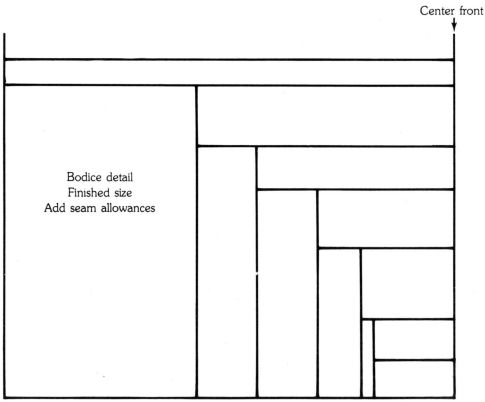

Bodice detail
Finished size
Add seam allowances

DRESDEN PLATE SKIRT
DESIGNED BY CHARLOTTE PATERA.
Color photograph on pages 106-107.

Prints run the full range of the spectrum in the Dresden plate blocks that circle this long gathered skirt. You will need four Dresden plate blocks to make a skirt. To make one Dresden plate, cut 1 circle and 15 wedge shapes, given here, for each pieced block. Join the wedge shapes and appliqué the circle over the center, covering the raw ends of the wedge shapes.

Appliqué the Dresden plate block to a white background fabric. Cut out the enlarged Dresden plates, allowing ¾″ of white fabric to extend past the appliquéd plates. Turn under the outside raw edges of the plate pieces, allowing ½″ of white background fabric to show. Appliqué the Dresden plate blocks around the bottom of the skirt, centering them at front, back, and sides.

A diagram for cutting a simple skirt is given here. The skirt can be gathered onto a band that is cut to your waist measurement plus overlap and seam allowances.

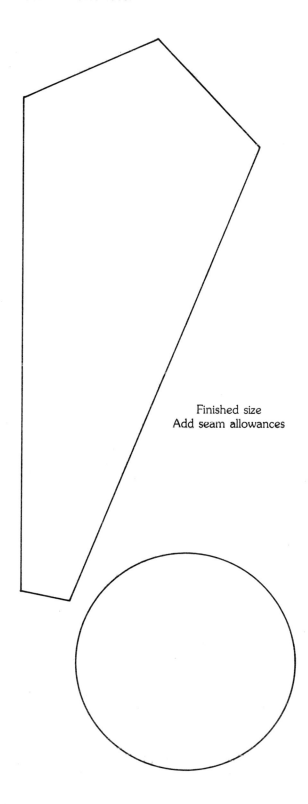

Finished size
Add seam allowances

27″

43″

31″

MONKEY WRENCH SKIRT

DESIGNED BY JOANNE DOUGHERTY.
Color photograph on pages 106-107.

The monkey wrench pattern makes an active, allover design on this wraparound skirt in which the pieced blocks alternate large and small polka dots, both in a brown and beige cotton and polyester blend. The traditional monkey wrench pattern is given here. This design depends upon a pattern of dark and light colors to make the monkey wrench motif appear.

Make up your patchwork of the monkey wrench to make a pieced fabric as large as your pattern. Cut according to your pattern. Cut a lining from a solid or print of a related color.

The pattern given here (medium size) is one that can be adapted if you intend to make a skirt from a ready-made quilt. Check for length. The sides and bottom edges can be bound with a bias binding, since the quilted fabric is too bulky to be stitched and turned.

For the waistband, cut two 84″ lengths of fabric. Join all edges except 35″ in center of one side. Center band on skirt, sew right side of waistband to skirt, and slip-stitch inside closed.

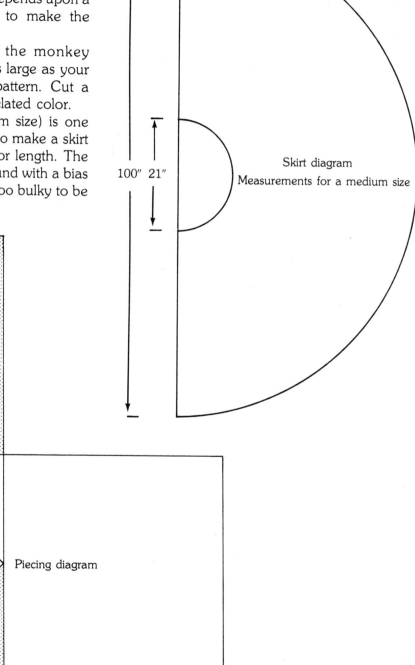

100″ 21″

Skirt diagram
Measurements for a medium size

Piecing diagram

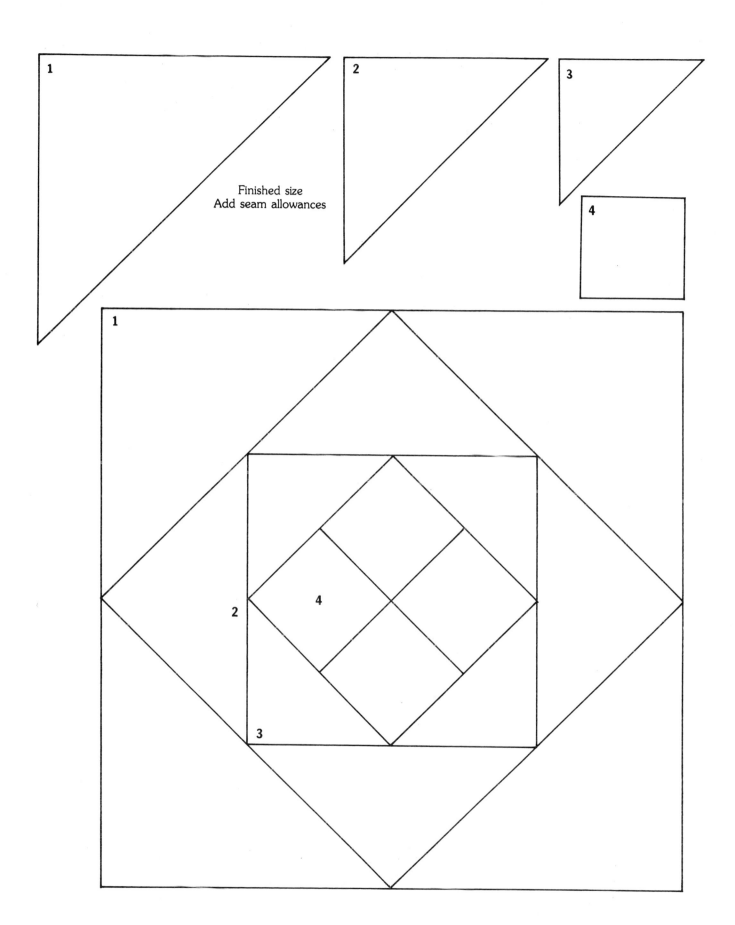

Finished size
Add seam allowances

DOILY JUMPER

DESIGNED BY JEAN RAY LAURY.
Color photograph on page 104.

Nostalgia-laden doilies and laces grace this country jumper. Doilies from the attic become flowers with the addition of organdy leaves and, in some cases, backings of organdy. The delicate, frosted look results from a combination of hand sewing and machine appliqué.

The skirt is made from a width of fabric (selvedge at waist and hem) so it can be whatever fullness you wish. Lay the material out flat and arrange the appliqué. Cut stems and leaves from cotton organdy and stitch with white thread in a machine satin stitch. Tack the doilies in place with tiny catch stitches.

PIECED AFRICAN SHIRT

DESIGNED BY BERTIE BOOTH.
Color photograph on page 104.

The simplest form of the pullover garment is a rectangle with a hole in the center. The poncho is the most familiar pullover of this type. This pullover is nearly square and is sometimes called the African Shirt. Many ethnic tops are made from this simple shape, some with side seams.

The material in this poncho is made up of pieced strips varying in width from 2″ to 7″ wide, with a few larger pieces. Join the strips with ½″ seams, right sides facing, and press to one side. Complete enough patchwork to cut a 44″ square. Cut a 6″-square in the exact center for the neck opening. Try on and adjust width or length as necessary. A second piece of fabric, cut the same size, is used for the lining. Place lining over patchwork, right sides facing. Line up edges and pin or baste. Sew the neckline opening. Trim and clip. Turn right side out and press.

Sew a running stitch or quilting stitch by hand about ⅜″ from the edge of the neck opening, using #8 perle cotton. Baste outside edges of pullover together. Bind raw edges with a strip of straight-cut binding (page 4). Cut the strip 1¼″ wide and turn under ¼″ seams so that the finished width is ⅜″. Quilt along patchwork seams with the same stitch and thread as that used around the neckline.

This pullover has streamers at each corner. Each streamer is made of four narrow ribbons 15″ long, knotted at one end and stitched to the corner.

MAN'S SHIRT

DESIGNED BY CHERYL GREIDER BRADKIN.
Color photograph on page 109.

This man's shirt utilizes a range of beiges, tans and white in the Seminole patchwork on cuffs and yoke.

Any shirt pattern can be used. If there is no front yoke, simply set the patchwork in to suggest a yoke. No padding and no quilting are used in this shirt. Patchwork is applied to the shirt during construction and is backed with the main shirt fabric. Use a variety of Seminole patchwork strips (page 17), alternating them with straight bands of fabric. In this example, the front of the yoke has two patchwork bands set between multiple straight bands of solid color.

SUNFLOWER JUMPER

DESIGNED BY JEAN RAY LAURY.
Color photograph on page 104.

A bright sunflower grows colorfully on the bib of this simple jumper. The finished sizes of the circles should be 9″, 7½″, 4⅜″, and 3½″ in diameter. Add seam allowances and cut one of each. Cut 16 petal shapes. First, appliqué largest circle to the bib piece; then stack and sew next largest circle on top. Pin petals in place, and then pin the next circle on top. Be sure all raw ends of petals will be covered by the circle when it is hemmed. Sew petals, and then sew two last circles. Our example is made from Mexican cotton and kettle cloth, and the appliqué is whipstitched.

Petal
Finished size
Add seam allowances

Finished size
Piecing pattern

Appliqué for bodice
Finished size
Add seam allowances

C

C

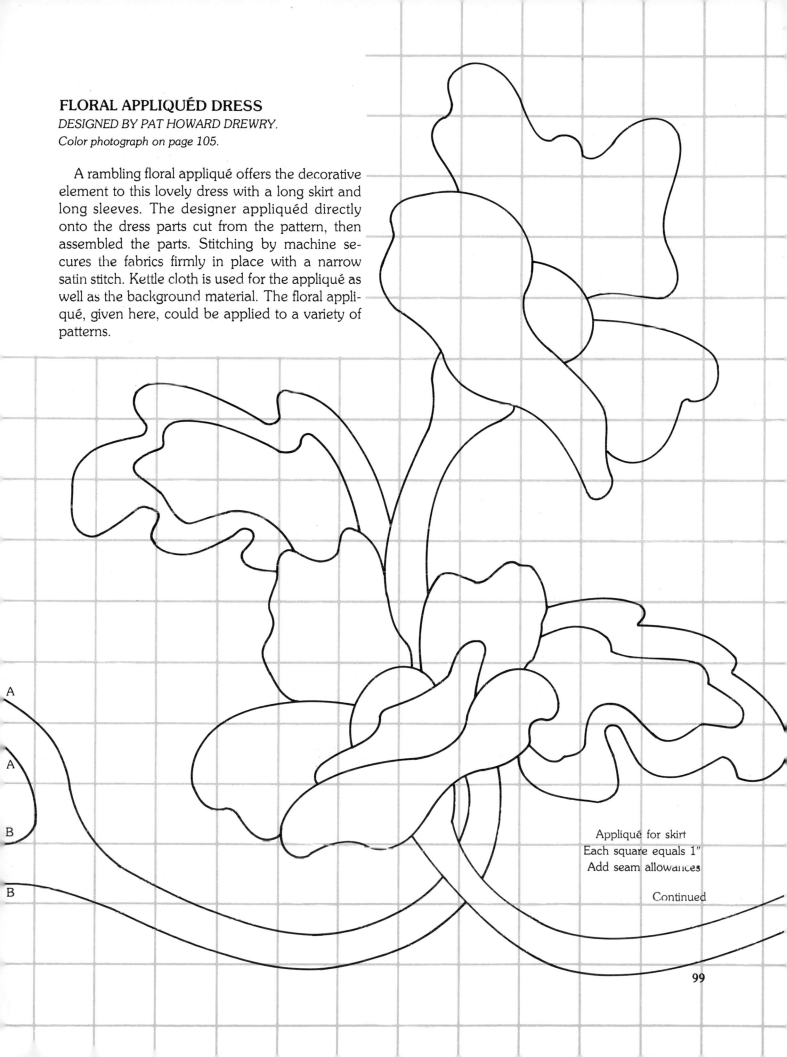

FLORAL APPLIQUÉD DRESS

DESIGNED BY PAT HOWARD DREWRY.
Color photograph on page 105.

A rambling floral appliqué offers the decorative element to this lovely dress with a long skirt and long sleeves. The designer appliquéd directly onto the dress parts cut from the pattern, then assembled the parts. Stitching by machine secures the fabrics firmly in place with a narrow satin stitch. Kettle cloth is used for the appliqué as well as the background material. The floral appliqué, given here, could be applied to a variety of patterns.

A

A

B

B

Appliqué for skirt
Each square equals 1"
Add seam allowances

Continued

99

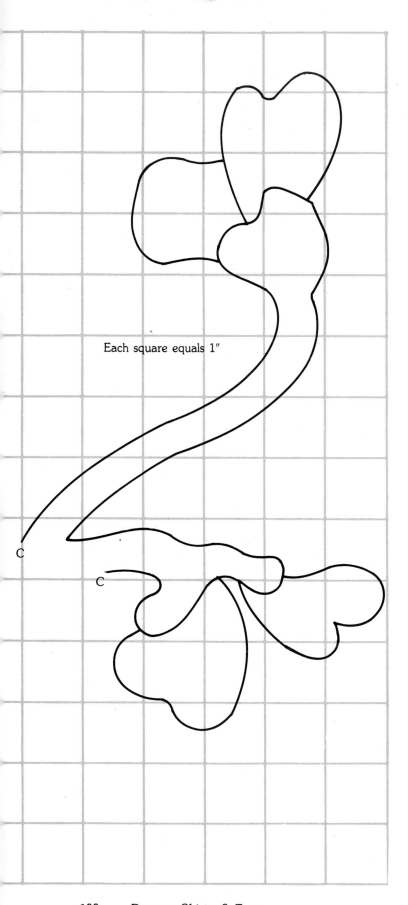

Each square equals 1"

C

C

MISSOURI BOATMAN'S SHIRT
DESIGNED BY MARLENE HEINZ.
Color photograph on page 103.

This handsome shirt is made from a Folkwear pattern. (See References, page 150.) Contrasting fabrics for cuffs, gussets, bindings, and collar add richness, while buttons offer a wonderful and amusing change of texture. The navy and print fabrics are appliquéd by machine to the shirt front. Their edges are then covered with straight-cut binding and topstitched. All appliqué, bindings, and buttons are finished before joining garment parts.

MAN'S SEMINOLE PATCHWORK SHIRT
DESIGNED BY CHRIS WOLF EDMONDS.
Color photograph on page 103.

A cream-colored Oxford cloth shirt is enriched with white-on-white Seminole patchwork. To embellish a man's shirt in a similar way, start with any favorite or well-fitting shirt. Open the neckband seam and the sleeve seams; then lay the shirt out so that back yoke and front of shoulders lie flat. Cut a pattern to cover back yoke, shoulders, and upper front of shirt.

Make three bands of white muslin Seminole patchwork (page 17). To vary the appearance of the shirt, you may want to try bright colors in the Seminole patchwork for a more casual effect.

Connect the bands of patchwork with narrow strips of muslin; then cut to fit your yoke-shoulder pattern. In the shirt shown here, the new back yoke is 2″ deeper than the original one, with the additional 2″ extending down the back of the shirt.

A front yoke is created by overlapping the patchwork from the shoulder onto the upper shirt front. Stitch the patchwork shape over the fabric yoke and shoulders of the shirt by turning under the raw edges and stitching the edges by hand in the front and back of the shirt.

Sew the neckband and the sleeve seams on original seam lines, catching all the raw edges of the Seminole patchwork in those seams to finish the shirt.

OHIO STAR DRESS

DESIGNED BY CHARLOTTE PATERA.

Color photograph on page 103.

The Ohio star and flying geese quilt blocks combine to form a stunning pattern on this orchid kettle cloth dress.

Select any simple dress pattern with a square neckline. The square neck opening should be the same width as your finished Ohio star block.

The Ohio star and flying geese quilt blocks are given here. For the average long dress, you will need 8 Ohio star blocks for the center panel and 36 flying geese blocks for each side panel. When blocks are complete, join the Ohio stars to make a long band. Join the flying geese into two long bands and then join the three bands, matching seams and blocks. Finally, join these to the dress fabrics and cut according to garment pattern.

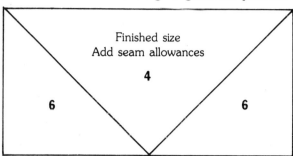

Finished size
Add seam allowances

4

6   6

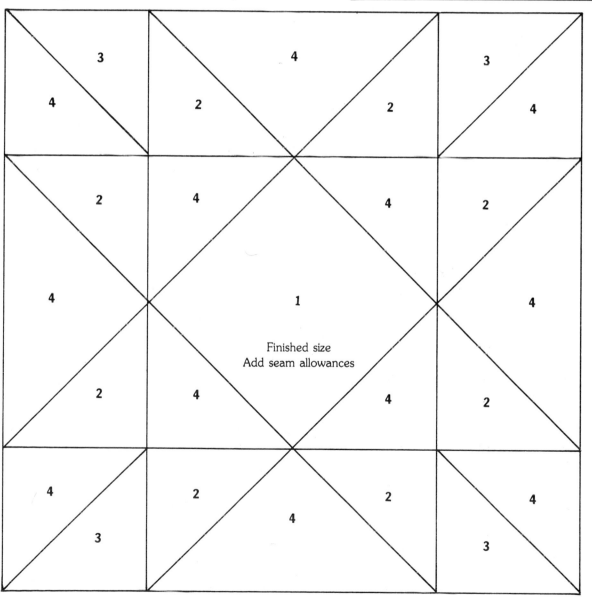

3   4   3

4   2   2   4

2   4   4   2

4   1   4

Finished size
Add seam allowances

2   4   4   2

4   2   2   4

3   4   3

BLUE DENIM JUMPER

DESIGNED BY JENNY BONYNGE.
Color photograph on page 103.

The ever-popular blue denim jumper is given an added fillip with a bodice pieced with an eight-pointed Ohio star. Use a jumper pattern with a simple bib and set in the pieced quilt block. Add triangles at top and bottom to achieve the necessary length for the bib top. Add a strip of the blue denim used in the garment to each side of the pieced center to form a panel of material large enough for the bib of the jumper. Topstitch to complete the design.

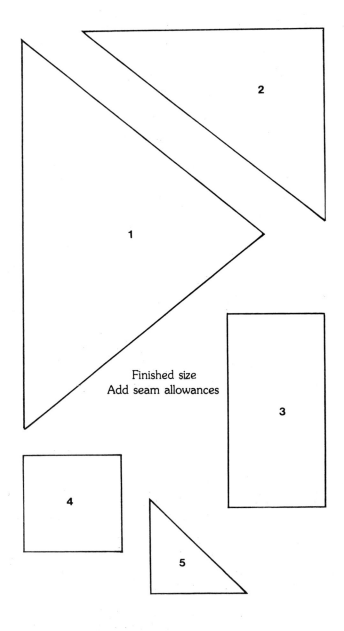

Finished size
Add seam allowances

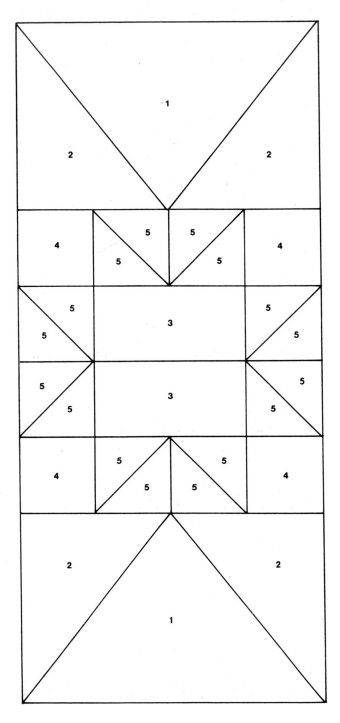

Clockwise from top:
MAN'S SEMINOLE PATCHWORK SHIRT, page 100;
MISSOURI BOATMAN'S SHIRT, page 100;
BLUE DENIM JUMPER, page 102;
OHIO STAR DRESS, page 101.

Left: DOILY JUMPER, *page 96.*

Below center: SUNFLOWER JUMPER, *page 96.*

Below left: PIECED AFRICAN SHIRT, *page 96.*

Right: FLORAL APPLIQUÉD DRESS, *page 98.*

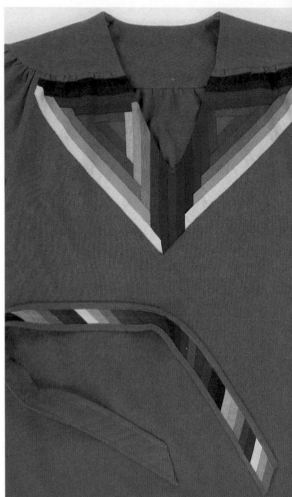

MAN'S SHIRT, *page 96.*

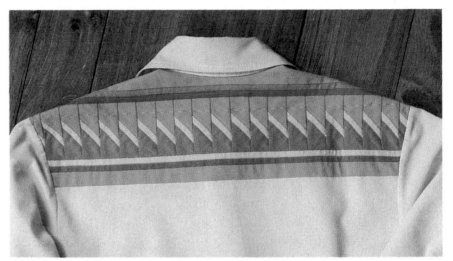

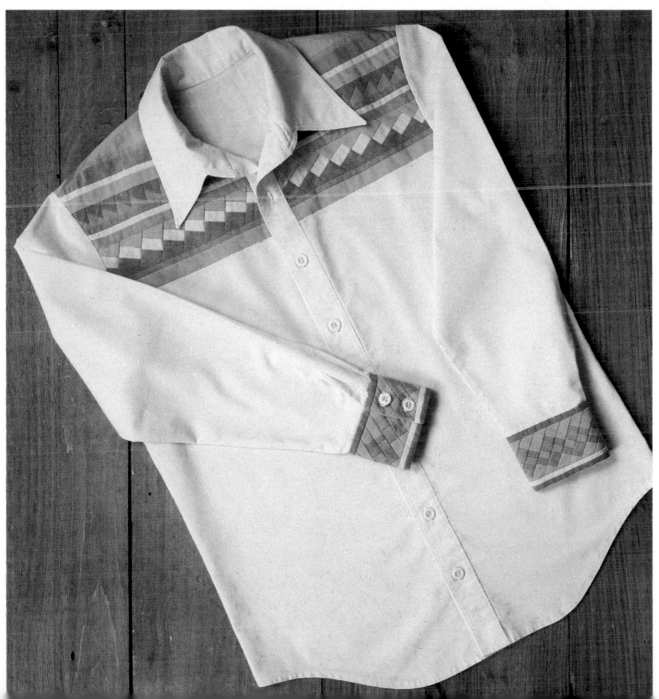

SILK WEDDING DRESS

DESIGNED BY BETTY MASON.
Color photograph on page 110.

Seminole patchwork, in white and off-white silks, makes the decorative bodice and sleeves on this wedding dress. The designer used the Nomad Dress pattern from Yvonne Porcella's *Five Ethnic Patterns.* The pattern is given here with permission. The effect could easily be duplicated on almost any dress pattern with a slightly raised waistline.

The yoke of this dress should slip loosely over the bust. To determine the width of the yoke, add 2 extra inches and ½" seam allowances to your bust measurement; divide in half for front and back. For a 36" bust, for example, add 36", 2" and 1", and divide by 2 for a width of 18½". For the length of yoke, measure from front to back from the point below the bust where you want the gathers to begin, over the shoulder, and down the back to a comparable length (about 24" for a medium size). Cut a rectangle to size. Cut a facing the same size. Place facing over yoke panel. Draw the V-neck opening, given in the diagram, onto the facing. Cut as indicated by the solid line of the diagram; stitch on broken line. Trim the seam. Turn, and baste raw edges together.

At this point, the yoke can be embellished with a variety of designs and techniques. For the dress shown in the photograph, bands of Seminole patchwork (page 17) are alternated with bands of plain silk.

The sleeves require rectangles the width of the yoke length (24" in this case) and the length of your arm from the shoulder edge to the wrist (about 20"); add seam allowances to width and length. Cut sleeves, and decorate as desired. For the silk Wedding Dress, the bands of Seminole patchwork are again alternated with strips of plain silk. Match shoulder line to top of sleeve line, right sides together, and sew.

The length of the skirt is determined by height and style. The mid-calf length shown in the photograph is about 33". For a full skirt, use 2 lengths

SILK WEDDING DRESS, page 111.

for the front of the dress and 2 for the back. Join front skirt panels. Gather skirt and sew to lower edge of yoke. Repeat for skirt back.

With right sides together, fold dress on shoulder line to form a T-shape. Sew underarm seam and side skirt seam. Hem sleeves and skirt.

As finishing touches, satin ribbons, sewn from the waistline, are capped off with tiny brass bells and stuffed hearts. Some of the hearts are stuffed with rose-scented potpourri; others are stuffed with scented batting.

A wreath for the bride's head is made of stuffed bands of silk that are braided together. Ribbons cascade from each end of the wreath, and each ribbon ends in a stuffed heart.

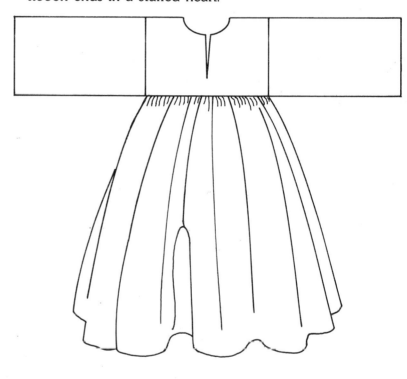

Vertical center of yoke

◄4½"-5" width► — Horizontal center of yoke

6"

Solid lines indicate cutting lines

Broken lines indicate seam line

PATCHWORK YOKE DRESSES
DESIGNED BY MARIA MCCORMICK-SNYDER.
Color photographs on page 108.

Three dresses, all made from a V-necked pattern with very simple lines, become unique through their original treatments for the necklines. Each uses a variation of strip piecing in log cabinlike patterns, one of which is given here. The strips overlap so that the raw edges are always covered, and the final edge is stitched in place by machine.

The dresses are made of suedelike fabric. Cotton fabrics make up the log cabin designs. Start with the diamond shapes that form the center of the log cabin and add strips, alternating as you work out from the center.

3

1

Finished size
Add seam allowances

2

3

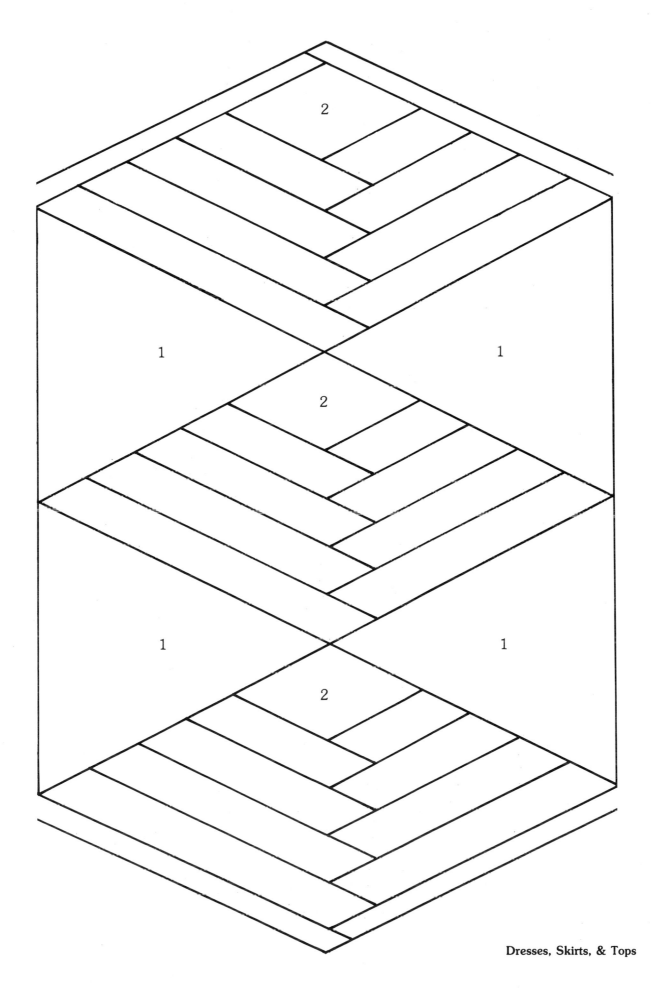

Children's Clothes

Watermelons, pigs, dragonflies, and buttercups invite children to run, jump, and tumble in these durable, quilted clothes. Here is an abundance of humor and bright color. Prints and patchwork are popular because wear and tear are less evident amidst all the activity of the pattern. One of the reasons it is fun to sew special togs for children is that they respond with enthusiasm and appreciation. Try one of these for a child you know.

CHILD'S LOG CABIN JACKET

DESIGNED BY WENDY PHILLIPS.
Color photograph on page 122.

A jacket this colorful cannot easily be left behind in the playground! The yellow-red-and-blue combination is heart-warmingly bright and splashy.

Using a straight-cut pattern, the designer made four log cabin blocks (page 16) for the front of the jacket and four for the back. To vary the size of the jacket, simply add more or fewer strips to the log cabin blocks. The sleeves of the jacket are strip quilted.

Warmth and puffiness are added through the use of batting. All edges are bound with the print used in the patchwork blocks.

DRACULA SKI VEST

DESIGNED BY MARY SOUZA.
Color photograph on page 122.

Using her child's drawings of Dracula, complete with fangs, the designer silk-screened the figures onto cotton/polyester fabric. The vest can be made from any child's jacket pattern; the yoke,

shown here, is simply adapted from the pattern (*see* Adapting a Pattern to Piecing, page 19).

Appliquéd figures, embroidery, or even fabric paints can bring your child's drawings into his wardrobe. The quilting pattern is an irregular zigzag line that relates both to the stars in the pattern and to Dracula's fangs.

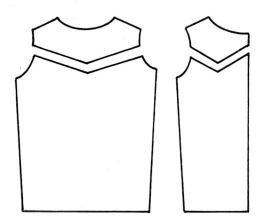

CHILD'S STRIP COAT

DESIGNED BY SONIA BERTSCH.
Color photograph on page 123.

Strip piecing (page 14) turns a simply-styled child's robe into a very special garment. Starting with a straight-cut pattern, the designer made up the coat in soft colors and prints. All edges are bound with a bias strip of blue, picked up in the blue print of the lining. Button loops (page 22) are made of cording in matching blue.

BOOTIES

DESIGNED BY SONYA BARRINGTON.
Color photograph on page 123.

Wonderful little quilted booties are made from a mattress pad. To make yours, first check foot size with the pattern for the sole, given here. Enlarge or reduce it in size as necessary, and alter other pieces accordingly. Exact fit is not necessary, since the booties tie.

Cut parts from mattress pad or prequilted material according to the pattern. Then cut bias strips from a printed fabric; allow approximately 34″ of bias strip for each bootie. Cut the bias 1" wide and take ¼" seams. Sew bias to heel section on three sides, placing right side of bias on top of heel section. Sew heel, sole, and bias from A to A. Turn bias, and whipstitch the raw edge by turning it under and stitching. Sew bias to double-curved edge of boot top, from B to B, finishing as for heel. Pin top to sole, starting at A on sole pattern. Take a small tuck in the top as indicated by C/D. Pin heel in place, overlapping it onto boot top at each side. Pin bias on top, lining up all raw edges, and sew through all layers at once. Turn bias to bottom of sole and hand stitch. Make hand buttonholes at spots marked with a circle. Make bias cording 18" long for each bootie. Thread the cording through the holes. Tie a Chinese ball knot (page 22) at the end of each, bringing raw ends back to cording to secure them.

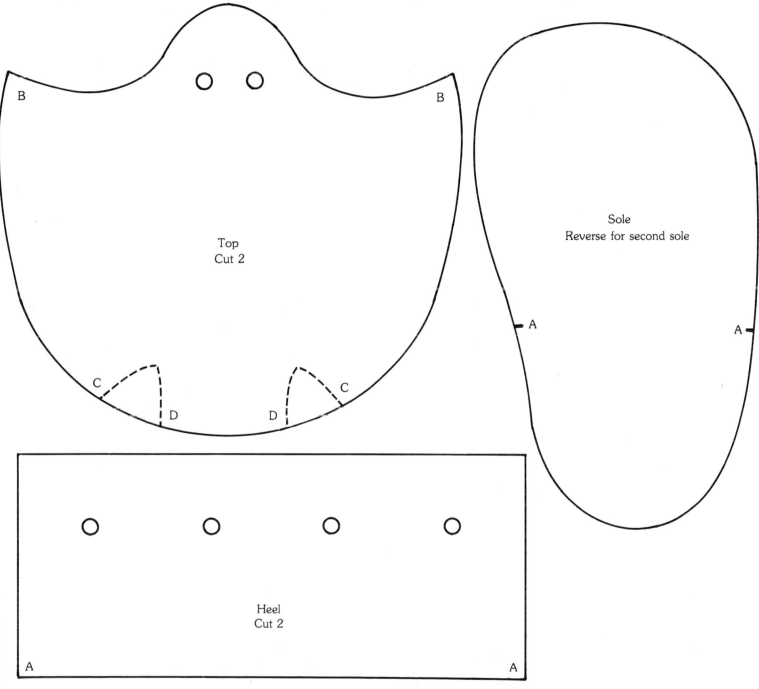

Top
Cut 2

Sole
Reverse for second sole

Heel
Cut 2

RAINBOW JACKET

DESIGNED BY THELMA JOHNSON.
Color photographs on pages 122 and 123.

This jacket is a big, wonderful, wearable watercolor painting! The designer made it for her grandson by painting directly onto polished cotton with fabric dyes.

On the back of the jacket, cows graze and apples grow as a sky writer flies his plane, writing "Nathan" in the summer sky. On the front, a rainbow sweeps across the body and onto the sleeve.

Various kinds of fabric dyes are available for direct-dye painting. Even permanent-color marking pens can be used effectively in a drawing on fabric.

Select a jacket pattern with a straight back panel. Bind the seams on the outside to frame the painting. Use quilt batting for the filler, and hand quilt with regular sewing thread.

Finished size
Add seam allowances

Repeat other leaf here

JUMPERS

DESIGNED BY RITVA LAURY.
Color photograph on page 120.

Ice cream colors make up into bright jumpers. The jumper begins with a basic pattern. Cut the pattern into sections, add seam allowances, and piece the sections in contrasting bright colors. Appliqué shapes given here are added to this single top layer of material. The front is then joined to the back at one side seam only. This single flat piece is then placed over a colored lining with a thin layer of polyester batting between. Quilting is hand sewn and follows the shapes of the appliqués. After quilting is finished, the second side seam is joined and finished on the inside. The bottom edge is hemmed and the neckline/arm opening is finished with a bias binding. Velcro® fasteners for the shoulders add to the practicality of the jumpers.

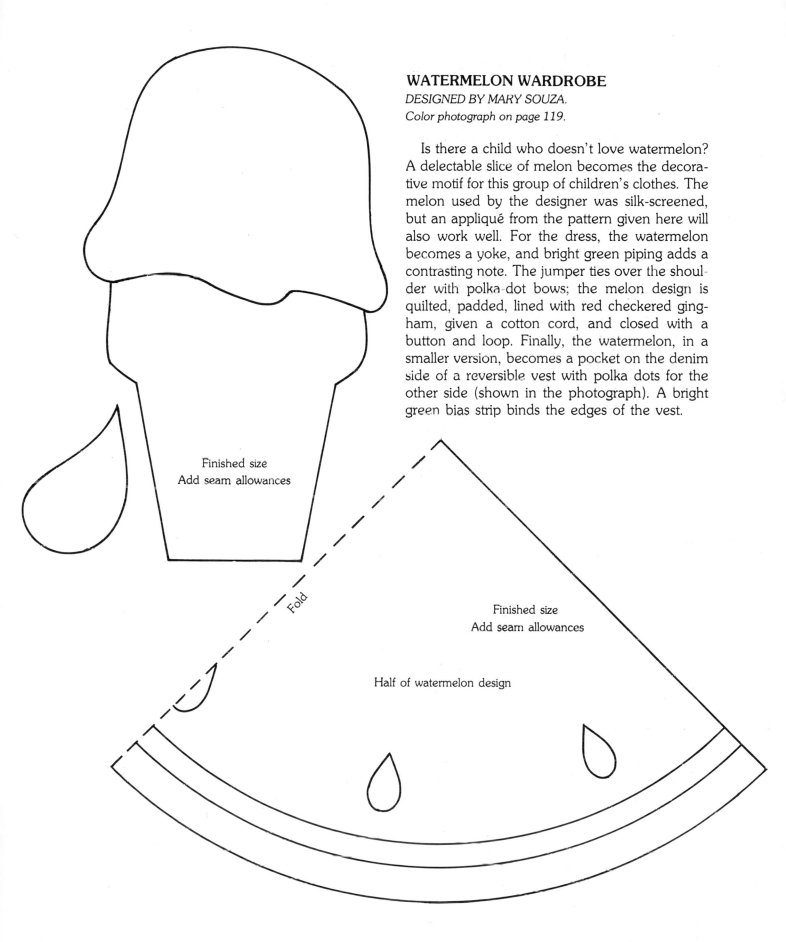

WATERMELON WARDROBE

DESIGNED BY MARY SOUZA.
Color photograph on page 119.

Is there a child who doesn't love watermelon? A delectable slice of melon becomes the decorative motif for this group of children's clothes. The melon used by the designer was silk-screened, but an appliqué from the pattern given here will also work well. For the dress, the watermelon becomes a yoke, and bright green piping adds a contrasting note. The jumper ties over the shoulder with polka-dot bows; the melon design is quilted, padded, lined with red checkered gingham, given a cotton cord, and closed with a button and loop. Finally, the watermelon, in a smaller version, becomes a pocket on the denim side of a reversible vest with polka dots for the other side (shown in the photograph). A bright green bias strip binds the edges of the vest.

Finished size
Add seam allowances

Fold

Finished size
Add seam allowances

Half of watermelon design

CHILD'S SUIT

DESIGNED BY GINGER JOHNSON.
Color photograph on page 119.

Quilting, padding, and rickrack combine to make an outfit that any child would love! It is the Turkish Tunic and Bloomers, Folkwear pattern #109 (see References, page 150), with these variations: The front has been zippered and the tunic shortened.

A thin layer of batting between tunic and lining gives it a soft fullness. Hand-quilted hearts enhance printed panels. An interesting detail is the way the bias binding covers half the rickrack along the edges, making a scalloped design.

FLEECY BANDANA COWBOY VEST

DESIGNED BY MARY SOUZA.
Color photograph on page 119.

Cowboy bandanas are cut to make the yokes of a wild-riding dude's vest, and a larger triangle of bandana is repeated on the back of the blue denim vest. The lining is acrylic sheep skin. Any vest pattern can be adapted to this design. Bandana corners are placed on top of the denim to give the effect of a yoke. Cording is slipped under the bandana, and cording and bandana are machine appliquéd directly to the vest. Red topstitching completes the design.

POLKA-DOT APRON

DESIGNED BY LYNETTE CEDERQUIST.
Color photograph on page 119.

The fanciful apron is made according to our simple pattern. Use any printed block, quilt block, or patterned fabric for the front medallion. In this one, a silk-screened block is appliquéd to the dress front, then quilted on all the lines.

A red polka-dot apron is sewn to a prequilted fabric used as lining. Right sides together, the apron front is sewn to front lining with an opening at hem. Repeat for apron back. Turn, slip-stitch shut, and join shoulder seams by hand. Ribbon ties are inserted under the printed block.

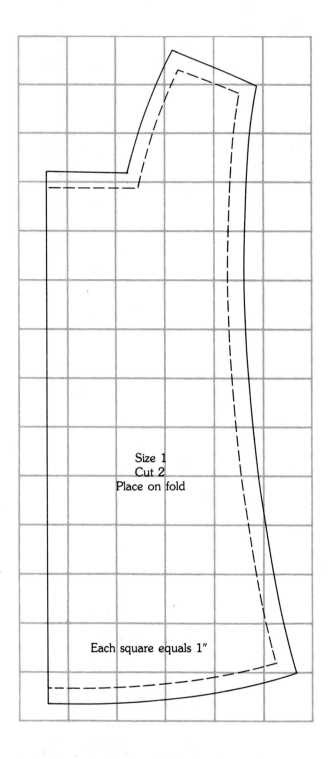

Size 1
Cut 2
Place on fold

Each square equals 1"

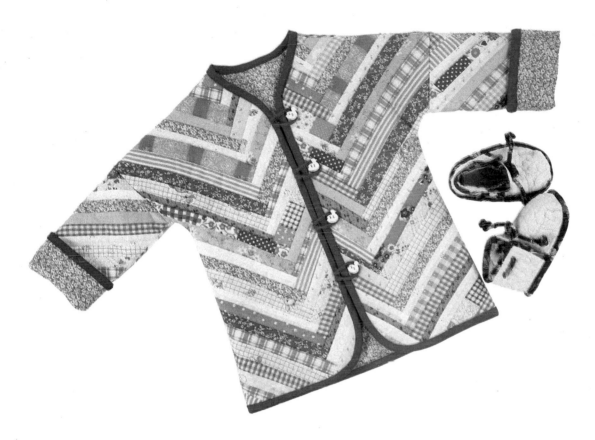

Above: CHILD'S STRIP COAT, page 114,
and BOOTIES, page 114.

Left, at Top: CHILD'S LOG CABIN JACKET, page 114;
bottom from left: DRACULA SKI VEST, page 114;
RAINBOW JACKET, page 116.

Below: RAINBOW JACKET, page 116.

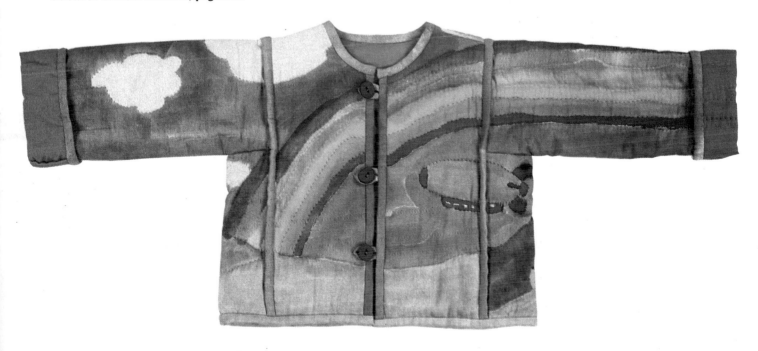

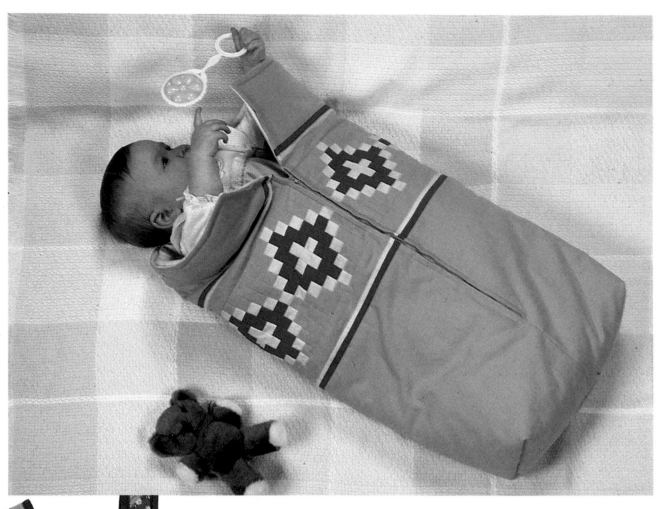

Above: BUNTING, page 125.

*Left: ROMPERS, page 125 and
BOY'S PLAYSUIT, page 125.*

BUNTING

DESIGNED BY LASSIE WITTMAN.
Color photograph on page 124.

The delightful baby bunting combines a quilted lining with a cover that is enhanced with a band of patchwork. This bunting is made from kettle cloth with solid lines of color to set off the patchwork. The band can be made from any patchwork or Seminole patchwork pattern.

Cut a 35"-wide × 30"-long rectangle of flannel lining and of bonded batting. Quilt flannel to batting, using a grid pattern with lines about 6" apart.

Cut the cover fabric to the 35" × 30" size. Assemble the patchwork or Seminole patchwork (page 17), and apply to the cover fabric, adding bands of solid fabric if desired. Join bag cover to lining, flannel side facing top of cover, leaving open the bottom edge and zipper area.

Insert a 16" zipper, starting 5" from the top edge. Box the bottom of the bag as shown in the diagram. Boxing seam should be 4" across corner. Finish by adding a row of topstitching across the top and to match the zipper topstitching. Add to length and width of the original rectangle to make a child's sleeping bag.

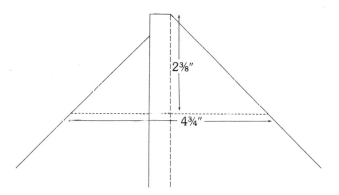

ROMPERS

DESIGNED BY JUDY FOSTER.
Color photograph on page 124.

Even the smallest portion of an old quilt can be utilized in clothing. In quilted rompers, the designer has used a section of quilt in combination with red velveteen. Our designer used a commercial pattern and added special buttons.

BOY'S PLAYSUIT

DESIGNED BY JUDY FOSTER.
Color photograph on page 124.

Old quilts often wear out in some parts, leaving other areas with miles of wear left in them. The designer of this playsuit used an old nine-patch quilt and a commercial pattern. All raw edges are bound in blue denim, and handmade buttons add a finishing touch.

PINAFORE

DESIGNED BY JEAN WELLS.
Color photograph on page 121.

The charming beribboned and pastel-colored pinafore is trimmed with laces and hearts. Made from cotton fabrics, the bib is the starting point. The square for the bib was cut chest size. The heart shape was reinforced with a fusible bonding web and placed on a white block. The entire block was then covered with organdy, giving a softness to the panel. Quilting stitches outline the heart. Strip piecing with ribbons and narrow strips of fabric was used to fill out the bib shape, with the muslin serving as a base fabric. The bib is lined.

The same technique was used in making the skirt border with hearts and more strip piecing. The skirt measures 90" around and is gathered at the top. The ruffle is double that: 180" around.

JUMPSUITS

DESIGNED BY JEAN RAY LAURY.
Color photograph on page 120.

The colorful, quilted jumpsuits are all variations of a simple pattern. In each, the fabrics are first pieced together; then the pattern parts are cut from this assembled fabric. The parts are placed over a muslin lining with a thin layer of polyester batting between. Straight line quilting is machine stitched on the flat pieces, using small quilting patterns on the bib sections and larger patterns on the legs. Quilting patterns are varied from one jumpsuit to the next.

Accents &
Accessories

If variety is the spice of life, this section offers an aromatic and savory reward. Many of these articles have no sizes, so they are great as gifts. Others, like the foot warmers and mittens, do not require specific sizing. Personalized details and decorative additions characterize most of the projects in this section. They offer a place and an opportunity to give vent to a flair that is not always wearable.

BOWTIE & BIRD NECKLACES
DESIGNED BY LYNNE SWARD.
Color photographs on pages 136-137.

The soft sculpture "pectorals" fit together like jigsaw puzzles. An added beauty of these necklaces is that they are reversible; flipped over, necklaces of a different color range appear.

For the bowtie necklace, cut bowtie shapes, given below, from different colors of silk. Fit the shapes together in various color arrangements to determine the final look. Each bowtie shape should be sewn from 2 colors of silk, so that the necklace shows a different color range when it is flipped over. In arranging the colors, consider placement for both sides of the necklace.

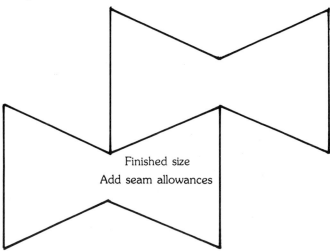

Finished size
Add seam allowances

Tiny machine stitches (15 to 20 to the inch) are needed to keep edges firm and avoid any fraying when the shapes are turned inside out. The stuffing must be smooth, consistent, and not overly full. Machine stitch the pairs of bowties together, right sides facing. Turn and stuff. Hand stitch the completed bowties to each other.

The bird necklace is made in the same manner as the bowtie necklace except that the birds are of different sizes and must be fit together in a particular sequence. Using the patterns given on page 127, cut backs and fronts for 2 #1 birds, 2 #2 birds, 2 #3 birds, 2 #4 birds, 2 #5 birds, 2 #6 birds, 6 #7 birds, 8 #8 birds, and 1 #9 backpiece. Assemble birds and hand stitch together in the sequence shown in the diagram below.

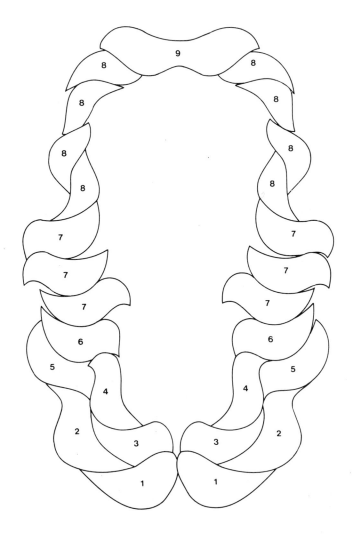

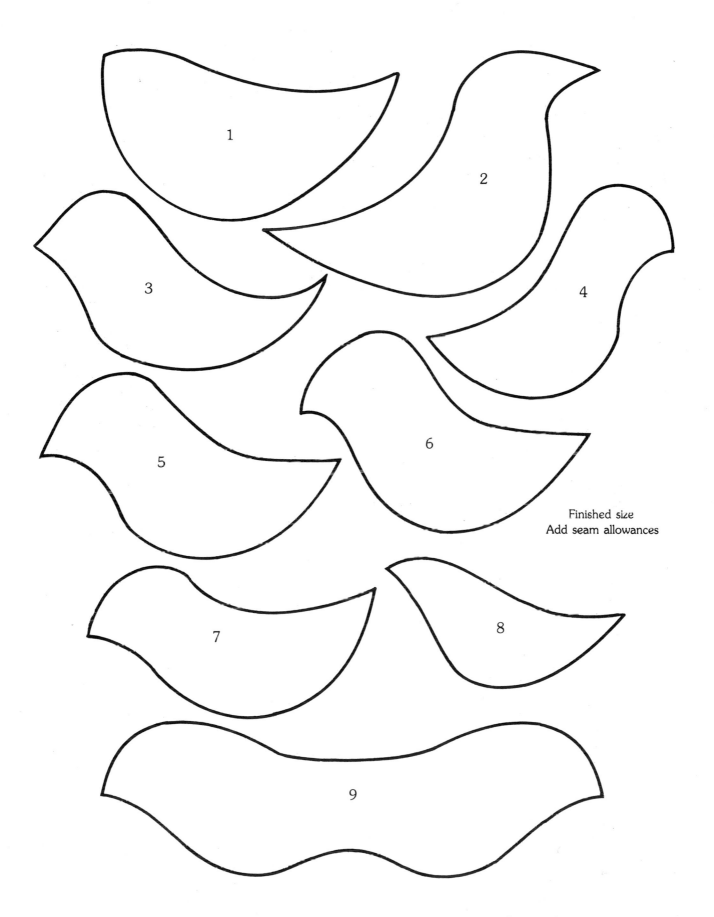

Finished size
Add seam allowances

HEART PENDANTS

DESIGNED BY MARINDA BROWN.
Color photograph on pages 136-137.

Embroidery and reverse appliqué are combined in these resplendent little heart pendants. The red one displays a strawberry plant at the center, embroidered with Russian punch needle or Igolochkoy on white fabric. Around the white heart shape is another in orange, a larger one in red and orange print, and a final heart in solid red. The brown heart is made similarly, combining patterns of brown fabric prints; at center is an embroidered lily. The tassel of one is made from perle cotton; the other is purchased. Macramé cord is used for the necklace.

To make a similar pendant you will need four squares of fabric, each 5″ × 5″. One of the colors should be white or light in color. Stack the four fabrics with the white on the bottom. Cut out the four heart shapes from paper. Center the largest paper heart shape on top of the fabric stack and trace around it with a chalk pencil. Baste on chalk line through all layers. Center the next largest paper heart over the first drawing and mark. Now draw up the center of the fabric so that you can cut into it. Allowing ¼″ seam allowance on the inside of the chalk line of the second heart, carefully cut out heart shape. The chalk line will be stitching line. Clip curves. Turn under seam allowance and slip-stitch to layer underneath.

Repeat with the other 2 paper hearts, centering each heart inside the last. Transfer the embroidery design to the center of the smallest fabric heart and complete, using embroidery thread. Add beads if desired. Then trim all layers, except the outer layer, to the basted edge. Remove basting. Trim outer edge to ½″ seam allowance and clip at very outside edge.

Using the largest heart as a pattern, cut a piece of cardboard to use as backing. Put a small amount of fiberfill on front of heart. Center cardboard, stuffing side against fabric. Pull edges of fabric around to back and glue in place. Glue cording to top of heart, and glue tassel to the point at the bottom. Again using the largest paper heart pattern, cut out a piece of matching felt to cover back surface. Glue in place.

Finished size
Add seam allowances

VARIABLE STAR APRON

DESIGNED BY ANN MORRIS.
Color photograph on page 139.

Variable star and squares-on-squares block patterns make this simple apron a stunning garment. Cut 2" squares of colored cotton fabrics; you will need 23 squares for the bib and two pockets. Use the color photograph and the diagram as a guide in arranging a balance of colored squares. Experiment to establish your own pattern if you wish.

To make a more complex design, as in this apron, four of the 2" squares on the bibs are made up of two colors each. (Figure 1.) The center square repeats the color of the adjacent

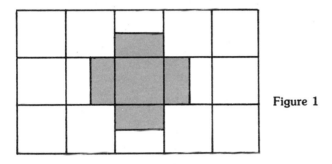

Figure 1

half of the pieced squares, allowing the "star" to appear when squares are added. (Figure 2.) To add these, cut 1½" squares; you will again need 23. Appliqué these smaller squares by hand to form diamonds in the center of each larger square, turning under ¼" and being careful to make points meet edges. Add a very small amount of batting, if desired, as you appliqué. Do not overstuff.

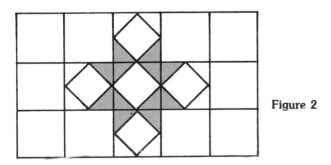

Figure 2

Make a single row of 4 squares for each pocket. (Figure 3.)

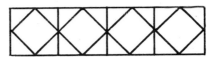

Figure 3

When the apron is assembled, hand appliqué the single rows of squares to the pockets. Then topstitch the pockets to the apron front. Appliqué the rectangle to the bib top. Add light batting if desired. Outline each of the smaller squares with quilting stitches.

TUNIC APRON

DESIGNED BY BLANCHE YOUNG.
Color photograph on page 139.

A handsome tunic features intricate Seminole patchwork and piecing. The designer cut her own tunic pattern. It is 12" wide at the neckline and increases to 22" in width at the lower edge. Using some of the methods described in her own book on *Lone Star Quilts* (See References, page 150), Blanche Young has made the yoke of radiating colors in postage-stamp blocks. The rest of the tunic alternates bands of Seminole patchwork (page 17) with plain and print fabric. Bias binding finishes all raw edges. Grosgrain ribbons make simple side ties.

DOWN BOOTIES

DESIGNED BY CORNELIA STEVENS.
Color photograph on page 138.

Down booties are wonderful for frosty mornings. This heart-patterned pair, complete with stuffed heart ties and polka dot lining, was adapted by the designer from a Frostline® kit for down booties, available at most sportswear shops. The designer added her own layer of lightweight fabric outside the kit's fabric, using French seams throughout. She suggests that you follow the kit pattern for sizes and for assembly instructions.

The tops of the booties are joined and quilted first. The bottoms are assembled separately, and then the tops are joined to the soles.

BOOTS

DESIGNED BY CAROL OLSON.
Color photograph on page 138.

Boots are wonderful for padding about the house on cool mornings or for snuggling into when thermostats are turned down. To make boots like these, cut according to the pattern given here, being sure to add seam allowances along cut edges. To adjust the pattern to another size, place foot on sole pattern, check measurements and adjust size if necessary. If you alter boots drastically, make up a muslin sample to check fit. Flip the sole pattern to have a right and a left boot for each pair.

Place cut boot parts on filler and backing so that parts can be quilted. A blanket makes a good filler, as does a layer or two of cotton flannel. Or use bonded quilt batt.

The blue velveteen boots were cut from this pattern. Quilt the leaf quilting pattern given here on sides before joining seams or adding lining. The rainbow-colored booties, also from this pattern, were made from 2"-wide pieced fabric strips which were quilted along the joining lines. A curve at the top adds a decorative touch.

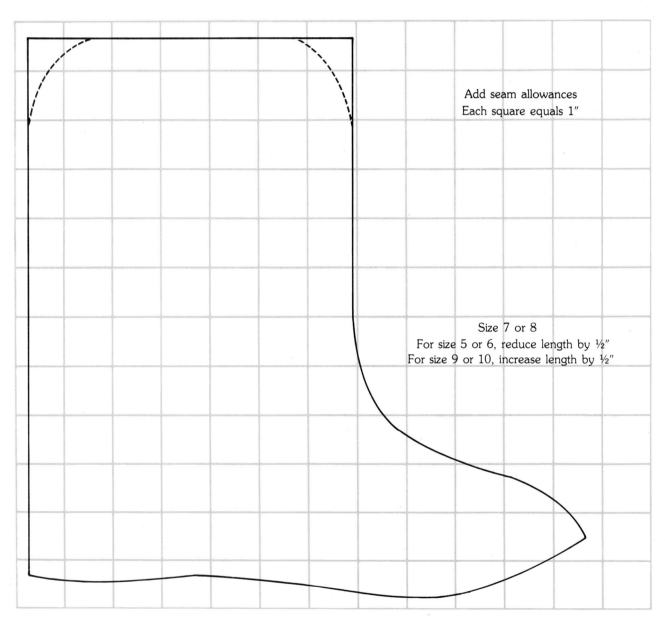

Add seam allowances
Each square equals 1"

Size 7 or 8
For size 5 or 6, reduce length by ½"
For size 9 or 10, increase length by ½"

Place right sides of outside fabrics together and stitch along back and front seams. Then join sole to boot sides, again with right sides facing. Clip and trim seams as necessary. Repeat for lining, taking a slightly larger seam. Join boot to lining, right sides facing, at top. Leave an opening of about 3″ in length at the back seam for turning. Turn through opening. Then slip-stitch the opening closed.

Boot straps are made from fabric cut 5″ long and 3½″ wide. Each strap is folded in half lengthwise, turned under, and topstitched or inserted in seam at the top edge.

Quilting pattern
Full size

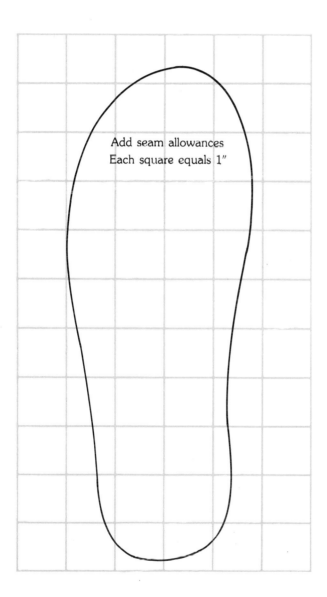

Add seam allowances
Each square equals 1″

MITTENS

DESIGNED BY CAROL OLSON.
Color photograph on page 138.

Mittens offer a marvelous opportunity for decorative appliqué and quilting. They do not require a great commitment in either time or materials, so they have a special appeal for the beginner. Design your own mittens of velveteen, corduroy, or printed fabrics. Try a pair with a different motif on the back of the mitten.

The pattern shown here has three parts. Drawings are given for a finished size, so be sure to add a seam allowance on each cut edge. The pattern can be adjusted for size. The one shown fits an adult. Make it shorter and narrower for a child. A muslin mock-up will assure correct fit. Do all the decorative piecing or appliqué on the back of the mitten before any assembly.

Cut one of each of the 3 parts for the right mitten. Turn the pattern over to cut parts for the left mitten.

To quilt, place each mitten part over filler. A bonded batt, blanketing, or flannel can be used. The filler will vary in weight, depending upon how thick or how warm you desire the mittens to

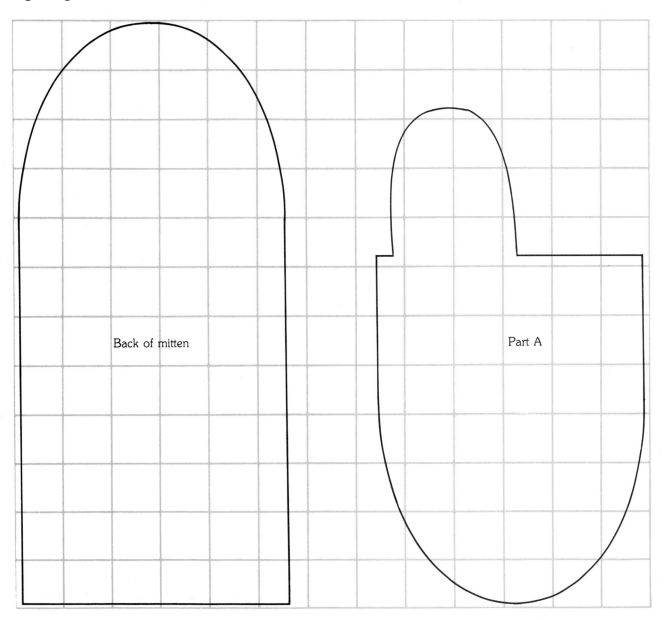

Back of mitten

Part A

be. Blankets make excellent filler, as do one or more layers of cotton flannel.

For the rainbow-colored mittens made from this pattern, cut strips of colored fabric 2½″ wide and join with ¼″ seams. Add a backing and filler, and lines quilt in next to the joining lines. Quilt the front, or inside, of the mitten in lines that follow the shape of the mitten.

The same pattern is used for mittens made of muslin and enhanced by a heart. Appliqué the heart to the back of the muslin mittens. Quilt around the heart. Quilt each section of the mitten separately.

When each part of the mitten has been quilted, join part A to part B, with right sides together, to form the thumb and inside of the mitten. Sew inside of the mitten to the back of the mitten. Trim seams, and clip at corners. Turn.

Cut the same pattern parts from lining fabric. Join the lining parts, leaving an opening at one side for turning. Then join the wrist end of the mitten to the wrist of the lining, with right sides together. Turn through the opening and slip-stitch together.

Finished size
Add seam allowances

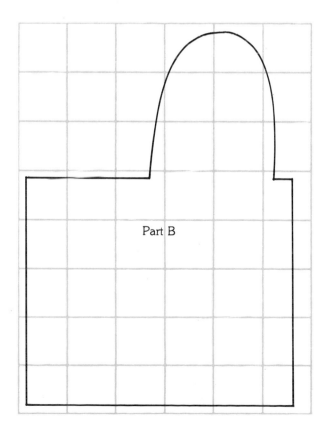

Part B

VELVETEEN CLUTCH
DESIGNED BY RITA ZERULL.
Color photograph on page 135.

A delicately detailed evening bag is made of velveteen and embellished with details in white and gold. Make a clutch using any simple pattern (or cut your own as our designer did). The velveteen bag measures 10″ across at the base and is 7″ high. This one uses a pieced section of the Dresden plate quilt block as the flap of the clutch. A Dresden plate block that could be adapted to this use is found on page 93.

A doily is also stitched to the flap of the bag, and embroidery with French knots softens the edge. A shisha mirror is set in and surrounded with boullion stitches. Then embroidery stitches in gold thread meander in soft swirls, picked up in a gold and white tassel. Gold hearts, lockets, and decorative gold beads add an elegant finish.

The simple lines of the quilting pattern radiate from the flap and emphasize the luxuriousness of the velveteen. Gold threads run through the white in the twisted-cord handle. An embroidered heart with a trail of French knots floats kitelike across the interior of the flap.

QUILTED CLUTCH

DESIGNED BY JUDITH A. HAROUTUNIAN.
Color photograph on page 135.

A simple and elegant clutch results from quilting on a rich velour surface. This one is machine quilted, but hand quilting can readily be substituted. Using the pattern given here, cut one piece from velvet and one piece from a lining fabric. Place right sides together and stitch along the outside edge, leaving an opening for turning. Turn, and slip-stitch closed.

This clutch has no filler, since the velveteen has so much cushion to it. If you are using a lighter fabric, add fleece or batting.

Hand baste on fold lines. Then machine quilt in any simple allover pattern, such as the rectangles used here. Topstitch the side fold lines to give a tailored, crisp edge to the bag. Next, with velveteen sides facing each other, join the side seams of the bag with a topstitch. Turn. Tuck side sections to the inside. Fold flap over front of bag.

CANVAS TOTE

DESIGNED BY MARILYN MCKIM HANNA.
Color photograph on page 135.

Quilting takes on new dimensions as a slightly plump ballet dancer pirouettes across this casual shoulder tote. The purse measures 12″ across and 13″ high.

A lightweight canvas is used for the tote, with a muslin backing and a polyester batting used as filler. Quilting is accomplished with machine stitches in a free-wheeling pattern as the designer "draws" with her sewing machine. The figure is given emphasis with a line of machine satin stitches. Only a rose in her teeth is sewn in color!

Lining is slipped into the bag and secured with binding added around the top edge. Strips 2″ wide are used to make the straps, which are knotted at the top to make the length adjustable. Straps are added last with machine topstitching. The tote is completely washable, providing all fabrics are prewashed before assembling.

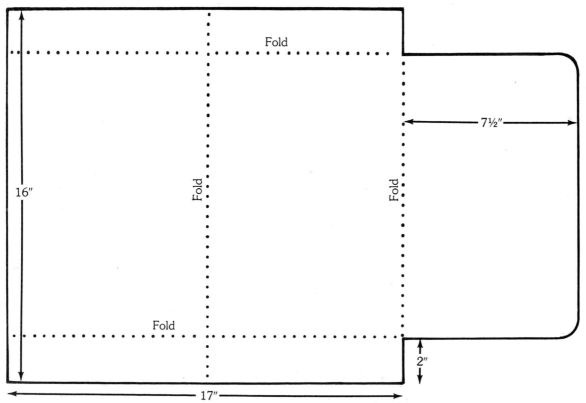

Clockwise from top left:
QUILTED CLUTCH, page 134; CANVAS TOTE, page 134; VELVETEEN CLUTCH, page 133.

Right: BOWTIE & BIRD NECKLACES, page 126, and HEART PENDANTS, page 128.

Top: EMBROIDERED SEMINOLE PATCHWORK BOOTS, page 144.

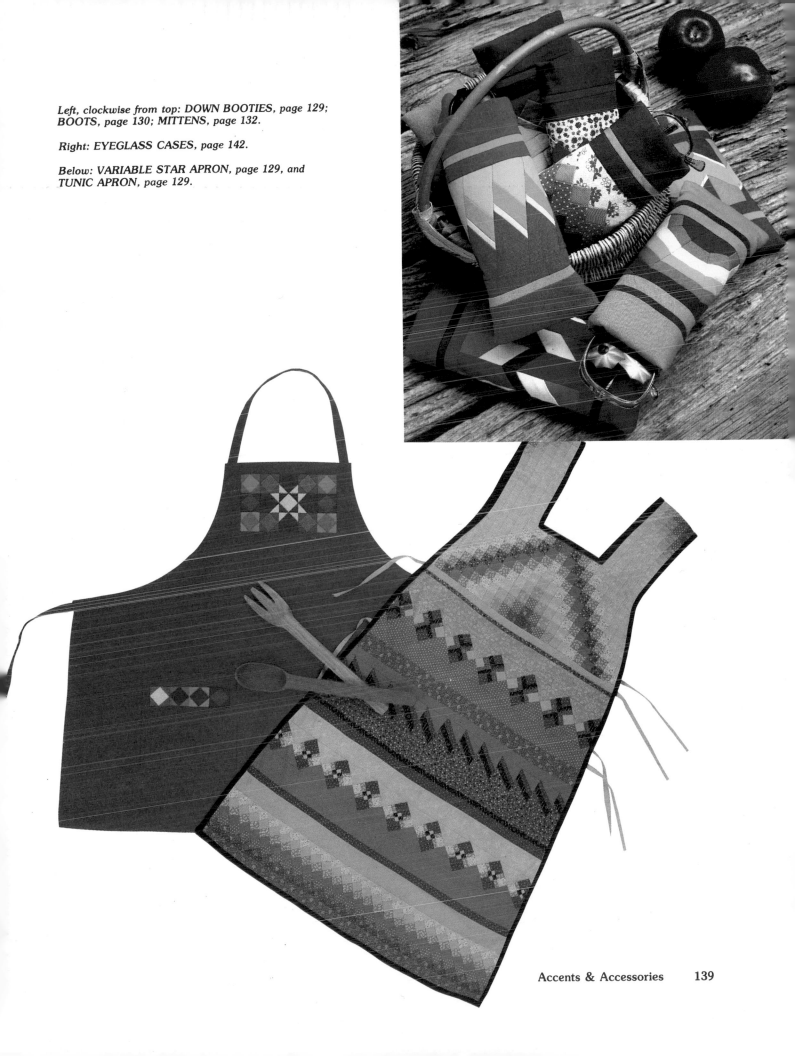

Left, clockwise from top: DOWN BOOTIES, page 129;
BOOTS, page 130; MITTENS, page 132.

Right: EYEGLASS CASES, page 142.

Below: VARIABLE STAR APRON, page 129, and
TUNIC APRON, page 129.

DOUBLE DIP T-SHIRT

DESIGNED BY ELLEN MOSBARGER.
Color photograph on page 140.

"Double Dip" offers an example of the ordinary T-shirt transformed into a special garment. A line of embroidery stitches in white perle cotton encircles the neck. The appliquéd ice cream cone design, from *P is for Patterns* by Ellen Mosbarger, is given here. (See References, page 150).

To apply the design to the T-shirt, first cut all parts according to the pattern, and pin them in place on the T-shirt. Dotted swiss and organdy are used on the example. Appliqué the sides of the cone. Add diagonal lines of embroidery, using couching or outline stitch. Sew sides and lower edge of the bottom scoop, overlapping it onto the top of the cone. Then add the top scoop, sewing all sides. Embroider along diagonal lines of the ice cream scoops, and, finally, appliqué the cherry on the top.

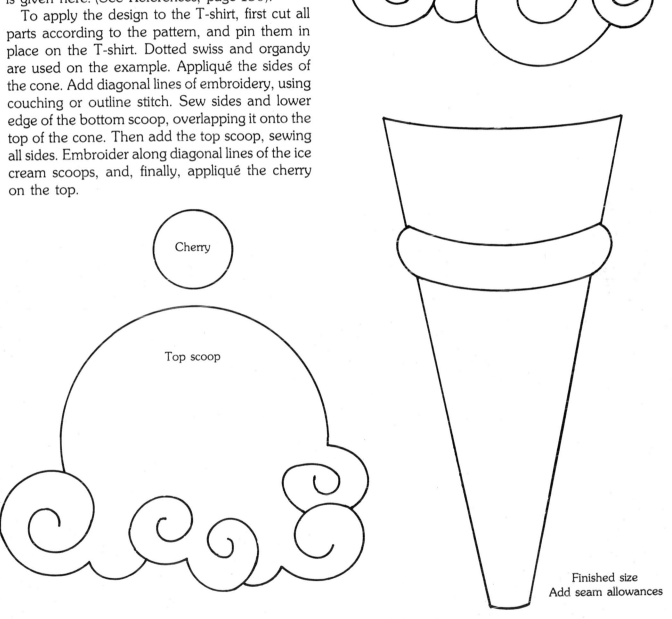

Bottom scoop

Cherry

Top scoop

Finished size
Add seam allowances

T-SHIRT, page 142, and DOUBLE DIP T-SHIRT, page 141.

T-SHIRT
DESIGNED BY ANN MORRIS.
Color photograph on page 140.

The ubiquitous T-shirt assumes a new personality when these unique appliqués, shown here, are added. The designer used all cotton fabrics, applying squares and circles of fabric to the neckline area in a necklacelike arrangement. Some of the shapes are lightly padded with batting, and a tiny running stitch secures them to the T-shirt. Embroidery stitches add minute details.

EYEGLASS CASES
DESIGNED BY LASSIE WITTMAN.
Color photograph on page 139.

Machine sewn and washable, each of these handsome eyeglass cases is individual and unique. They are made from a cotton and polyester blend.

The patterns are created with Seminole patchwork (page 17). Strips of fabric are joined, then cut into segments and rearranged. Each time there is a change in the width of stripes, color placement, or the angle of the cut, a new pattern is created.

For the case top, an 8¼″ × 3″-4″ decorative band of Seminole patchwork forms a center section; bands of fabric are added on each side of this band to form the 8¼″ square that is needed for the top.

For the center section of the blue and green case in the foreground of the photograph, first assemble straight strips as indicated in Figure 1. Then, following Figure 2 and the general instructions for Seminole patchwork, page 17, cut the straight strips with seam allowances and assemble as shown in the center section of the figure. Add

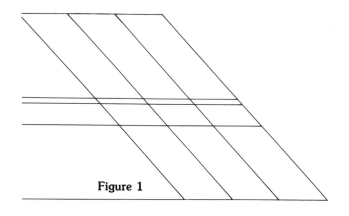

Figure 1

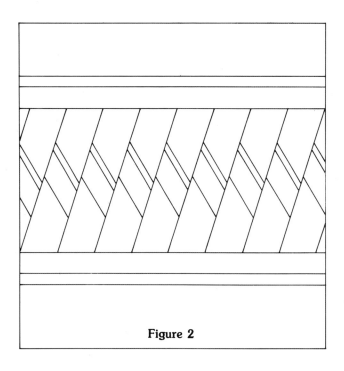

Figure 2

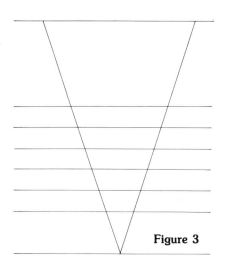

Figure 3

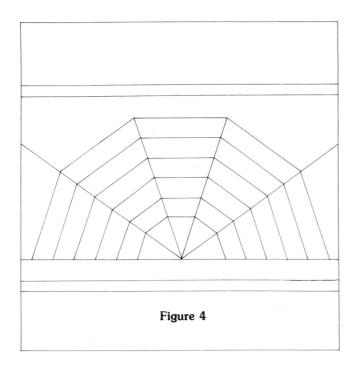

Figure 4

¼″ wider on both sides of the case. Sew all three layers at top seam only. Trim batting out of seam allowance.

Place case on table, batting side down. Gently pull lining out of the way so you can fold right sides of the case and lining together, matching decorative bands, and pin in place. At this point you will have a long narrow case. (Figure 5.)

Place one more pin at top seam line and fold back lining to back side of case. Lining fabric at top seam will extend ¼″ beyond case but should line up perfectly at bottom edge. (Figure 6.) Sew up side seam; back tack at end. Trim batting from seam allowance.

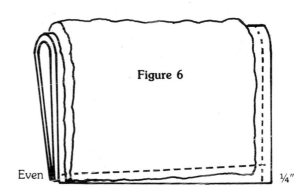

Figure 6

Even   ¼″

It is necessary to turn the case inside out. Hold only the part of the lining that is touching the batting and turn inside out. Match all fabrics at bottom edge (some adjustments may be necessary). Adjust the body of the case to fit neatly inside the lining, side seam at one side and folded fabric on other side. Pin and sew up bottom, using ¼″ to ⅜″ seam. Trim. Turn right side out and pull out at corners.

the straight bands on either side of the pieced band.

To make the eyeglass case with the bands that evoke a sunset, assemble a straight band of striped material. (Figure 3.) Cut triangles (allowing seam allowances) of the striped material as shown. Join triangles and add straight bands to complete the square. (Figure 4.)

To finish the case, place the decorative square, right side up, on top of batting, trim and pin all four sides. Place the 9″-square lining on top of the case top, with right sides together. Pin at top edge, through all three layers. Trim lining to match top and bottom edge of case, but keep it

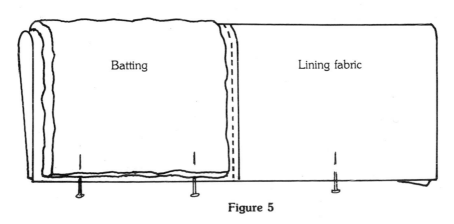

Batting   Lining fabric

Figure 5

EMBROIDERED SEMINOLE PATCHWORK BOOTS

DESIGNED BY MARGARET BOWMAN.
Color photograph on page 136.

This foot covering allows us a fantasy step with one foot in ethnic traditions and the other foot in a contemporary statement. Detailed embroidery and the dramatic colors of the piecing make these boots unique and beautiful.

Seminole patchwork is used to make up some sections that contrast to bands of solid velours. This play of plain stripes against fabrics that are literally encrusted with French knots and exquisite embroidery adds immeasurable richness.

Perhaps these will inspire you to try your own version. The designer's pattern to fit a medium (7-8) foot, is given here. Adjustments in size may be necessary for each wearer.

To make the sole of the boot, cut a sole shape first from velour; then topstitch 1"-wide strips of leather crosswise onto the sole for durability. Leave a seam allowance on the velour sole; cut leather strips to fit the finished area of the sole as shown.

For the top of the foot, assemble by machine a rectangle of three velour strips slightly larger than the pattern for the top of the foot section. Place pattern on rectangle and cut top of foot piece with seam allowance. Add desired embroidered detail.

For the spacer, cut a velour strip ⅞" wide plus a seam allowance and long enough to go around the perimeter of the sole. This piece is not decorated.

For the heel, sew together by machine three strips of velour sufficient to cut out a rectangle 2⅛" × 11¾" with seam allowance. This section is not decorated.

For leggings, assemble by machine a variety of Seminole patchwork bands of narrow (½" to 1") strips of velour. Overlay Seminole patchwork with embroidery detail. When all embroidery is finished, machine sew flat piece into a tube, 11" high and 17" around.

When all the parts are constructed and cut to size, the boot is assembled:

Using a machine, sew the 2 ends of the spacer together to form a circular band. Sew the spacer to the velour layer of the sole.

By machine, sew the top of foot to the open edge of the spacer, aligning the sole toe with the top toe. Connect the heel section to the spacer and top of foot by hand stitching on the wrong sides. This completes the foot of the boot.

With right sides together, hand sew bottom of legging to top of foot section.

Construct a lining of cotton broadcloth of undecorated pieces cut from patterns with seam allowances. The heel section may be cut in one piece. For added warmth and comfort, cut a piece of batting the size of the finished sole and tack it in place with hand stitches to the wrong side of the lining sole.

Turn lining, wrong side out and insert in boot. Connect legging lining and top of legging with a circular band of lining material stitched by hand to the lining, then folded down over outside of legging and stitched to outside.

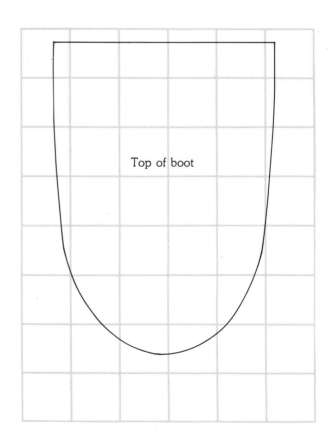

Top of boot

Side of boot

Place on fold

Each square equals 1"

Sole of boot

Designers' Gallery

Our gallery is a showcase for a collection of special, one-of-a-kind apparel. It is the purpose of this chapter to inspire you, to excite your imagination, and to energize your approach to sewing.

These designers have incorporated wonderful and unique decorative elements into their special pieces, and seeing them will trigger ideas for your own works. Most of the work in this section is designed by women with backgrounds of work in fiber and fabric arts. Many are more complex than what you may want to tackle on a first try. But this collection of attire will influence and stimulate your imagination for projects just now emerging in idea form.

VELVET BIRD VEST
DESIGNED BY ELLEN EDITH.

A beautifully quilted bird medallion is airbrush painted on cotton fabric, placed over polyester quilt batting and a backing, outline quilted with machine stitches that echo the bird shape, and set onto the vest. If our designer's airbrush technique is outside your range of experience, use a printed fabric, appliqué the bird, or, perhaps, color your own medallion with permanent-color marking pens or fabric paints.

GOLD MOLA VEST
DESIGNED BY SKYE JOHNSTONE.

Gold Mexican cotton, lined with pink, makes a brightly contrasting ground color for this garment. The outside of the vest is appliquéd with molas from the Cuna Indians of the San Blas Islands off the coast of Panama. On the back of the vest, another mola is set in with ribbon and ties. Coins and decorative bangles complete the design.

PURSE
DESIGNED BY GERDA RASMUSSEN.

In this museum of a purse, silver beads, ornaments, bangles, medals, pins, and awards add a touch of opulence over handwoven fabrics, velvets, and satin ribbons. Shisha mirrors, needle weaving, and embroidery add further detail.

SHORT JACKET & SIDE-CLOSURE JACKET
DESIGNED BY NANCY PAPA.

An interesting feature of both of these jackets is the metamorphosis that occurs when the sleeves are removed to form vests. A combination of buttons and zippers makes the sleeves removable. The Short Jacket also is made distinctive by a second pattern of quilting imposed on the sleeves that were cut from a prequilted fabric. The Side-Closure Jacket has medallions of the sleeve fabric appliquéd to the front.

HAORI
DESIGNED BY DIANA LEONE.

Batik fabrics and Japanese prints are combined with outline quilting in this jacket that becomes a vest when the sleeves are unbuttoned. The quilting outlines images in the painted materials.

FANTASY MUFFLER
DESIGNED BY SUZI ANDERSON BLUCHER.

A fancy fantasy it is to wrap in so elegant a muffler with colors that vary from navy to pale blue and gradually back again to navy. The piecing method is called Faceted Work and was developed by Marie Lyman, from whom our designer learned the technique. Each end of the muffler turns up to form a pocket.

KITE CLOTHES
DESIGNED BY NANCY CHAPPELL.

Using fabric paints, hand painting, hand drawing, and coloring with markers, the designer has created a glowing coat based on a traditional Japanese kite design. Ready-made cording provides the ties at underarm and at front. All raw edges are bound in bias strips. The "Sakata's Kite" skirt is another in this series of designs, and it, like the coat, is padded and quilted. Machine quilting echoes the drawn lines, exaggerating the color changes. A purse in the same design completes the outfit.

LOTUS CLOISONNÉ JACKET
DESIGNED BY GENNA PANZARELLA.

The elegance of jacket lies in the way the batik design, the quilting, and the shaping work together to make a perfect blend of the parts. The curved, shaped front is reflected in the sensuously curved row of satin buttons and the satin binding. This jacket is reversible. Another row of buttons is sewn to the satin side.

TIBETAN COAT
DESIGNED BY ROBIN JAMES.

To the basic pattern of the Folkwear Tibetan Coat, the designer added embroidery, machine appliqué, Seminole patchwork, log cabin, crazy patch, and satin stitch. She considers this her "sampler coat" and uses it as a walking example of the various techniques she teaches. Of special interest is the decorative panel down the back of the garment. Because of the weight of the piecing, no padding was used.

References

In this listing, you will find addresses for companies that supply patterns and booklets that are published by their authors.

Bradkin, Cheryl Greider. *The Seminole Patchwork Book.* Atlanta: Yours Truly, Inc., 1980.

Fanning, Robbie and Tony. *The Complete Book of Machine Quilting.* Chilton Book Co., 1980.

Folkwear Patterns, Box 3798, San Rafael, California 94902

Great American Cover-Up, 3213 Knox, Dallas, Texas 75205

Hoover, Doris and Nancy Welch. *Tassels.* Uno Graphics, Apple Tree Lane, 3505 Evergreen Drive, Palo Alto, California 94303

Johannah, Barbara. *The Quick Quiltmaking Handbook.* Pride of the Forest Press, P.O. Box 7266, Menlo Park, California 94025

Leone, Diana. Pieced Log Cabin Jacket Pattern. 2721 Lyle Court, Santa Clara, California 95051.

Mosbarger, Ellen. *P is for Patterns.* Calico Mouse, 924 Sespe Avenue, Fillmore, California 93103

Ota, Kimi. *Sashiko Quilting.* 10300 61st Avenue South, Seattle, Washington 98178

Porcella, Yvonne. *Pieced Clothing, Five Ethnic Patterns,* and *Plus Five Ethnic Patterns,* 3619 Shoemake Avenue, Modesto, California 95351

Puckett, Marjorie. *String Quilts & Things.* Orange Patchwork Publishers, P.O. Box 2557, Orange, California 92669

Rush, Bev, with Lassie Wittman. *The Complete Book of Seminole Patchwork.* Seattle: Madrona Publishers, 1981.

Wittman, Lassie. *Seminole Patchwork Patterns.* 2221 76th Avenue, Bellevue, Washington 98004

Young, Blanche. *Lone Star Quilts.* Young Publications, P.O. Box 925, Oak View, California 93022

Index

Designers

Betty Amador, Pieced Jacket, page 55; Man's Kimono, page 62.

Margaret Ana, Blue & White Jacket, page 50.

Sonya Lee Barrington, Mattress Jacket, page 48; Booties, page 114.

Sonia L. Bertsch, Child's Strip Coat, page 114.

Jinny Beyer, Tibetan Panel Coat, page 76.

Wendy Bloom, Blue Turkish Coat, page 77.

Suzi Andersson Blucher, Fantasy Muffler, page 148.

Jennifer L. Bonynge, Blue Denim Jumper, page 102.

Bertie Booth, Pieced African Shirt, page 96.

Barbara M. Bowers, Rainbow Log Cabin Vest, page 41; Heart Jacket, page 49; Pink Silk Kimono, page 71.

Margaret Bowman, Embroidered Seminole Patchwork Boots, page 128.

Cheryl Greider Bradkin, Seminole Patchwork Jacket, page 49; Man's Shirt, page 96.

Marinda Ann Brown, Turkish Coat, page 78; Heart Pendants, page 130.

Lynette Cederquist, Polka-Dot Apron, page 118.

Nancy Chappell, Kite Clothes, page 148.

Marie Chesley, Red Chintz Coat, page 78.

Sheila Cook, Poppy Vests, page 30.

Ann deWitt, Picnic Kimono, page 72; Child's Japanese Jacket, page 74.

JoAnne Dougherty, Monkey Wrench Skirt, page 94.

Pat Howard Drewry, Floral Appliquéd Dress, page 99.

Ellen Edith, Pieced Star Pullover, page 90; Velvet Bird Vest, page 146.

Chris Wolf Edmonds, Tulip Vest, page 38; Man's Seminole Patchwork Shirt, page 100.

Judy L. Foster, Sunflower Quilt Vest, page 38; Rompers, page 125; Boy's Playsuit, page 125.

Elzanna Gay, Velveteen Jacket, page 56.

Marilyn McKim-Hanna, Canvas Tote, page 134.

Judith A. Haroutunian, Quilted Clutch, page 134.

Marlene Heinz, Quilted Coat, page 77; Braid Trimmed Coat, page 77; Missouri Boatman's Shirt, page 100.

Cindy Hickok, Up-With-Women Vest, page 36.

Doris Hoover, White Trapunto Vest, page 44.

Jody House, Calligraphy Vest, page 40.

Shirley S. Huffman, Black Silk Kimono, page 71.

Esther Hughes, Log Cabin Tibetan Vest, page 40.

Robin James, Tibetan Coat, page 149.

Thelma Johnson, Rainbow Jacket, page 116.

Ginger Johnson, Child's Suit, page 118.

Skye Johnstone, Gold Mola Vest, page 146.

Holley Junker, Wind or Rain Cape, page 78.

Phyllis Klapproth, Clam Shell Vest, page 39.

Jean Ray Laury, Rainbow Vest, page 39; Child's Kimono, page 62; Doily Jumper, page 96; Sunflower Jumper, page 96; Jumpsuits, page 125.

Ritva Laury, Jumpers, page 116.

Diana Leone, Log Cabin Jacket, page 50; Log Cabin Coat, page 77; Haori, page 147.

Carol Martin, Evening Vest, page 43; Flower Appliqué Jacket, page 50.

Nancy J. Martin, Strip-Pieced Skirt, page 90.

Betty Mason, Silk Wedding Dress, page 111.

Maria McCormick-Snyder, Patchwork Yoke Dresses, page 112.

Lee McHose, Tropical Jacket, page 46.

Ann Morris, Variable Star Apron, page 129; T-Shirt, page 142.

Ellen Mosbarger, Double Dip T-Shirt, page 141.

Carol Olson, Mittens, page 132; Boots, page 130.

Kimi Ota, Sashiko Vest, page 29; Black Vest, page 61; Blue Jacket, page 61.

Genna Panzarella, Lotus Cloisonné Jacket, page 149.

Nancy Papa, Short Jacket and Side-Closure Jacket, page 147.

Charlotte Patera, Dresden Plate Skirt, page 93; Ohio Star Dress, page 101.

Wendy A. Phillips, Child's Log Cabin Jacket, page 114.

Yvonne Porcella, Tibetan Sleeveless Coat, page 87.

Patricia P. Porter, Green Silk Jacket, page 50.

Donna A. Prichard, Scroll Vest, page 35.

Marjorie Puckett, Fan Evening Coat, page 87.

Gerda Rasmussen, Purse, page 147.

Janet Shore, Tibetan Vest, page 73.

Mary Souza, Dracula Ski Vest, page 114; Watermelon Wardrobe, page 117; Fleecy Bandana Cowboy Vest, page 118.

Cornelia H. Stevens, Down Booties, page 129.

Eleanor Stickle, Flowered Star Vest, page 44.

Cindy Summerfield, Paisley Print Dress, page 92.

Lynne Sward, Label Vest, page 41; Bowtie & Bird Necklaces, page 126.

Jean Wells, Pinafore, page 125.

Maxine J. Winegarner, Butterfly Vest, page 42.

Lassie Wittman, Bunting, page 125; Eyeglass Cases, page 142.

Blanche Young, Tunic Apron, page 129.

Rita Zerull, Lacy Vest, page 43; Velveteen Clutch, page 133.

Senior Editor: Candace N. Conard
Editor: Jo Voce
Design: Viola Andrycich
Cover Photograph: John O'Hagan
Photography: John O'Hagan, all photography with the following exceptions: Mike Clemmer, top left page 32, page 53; Mac Jamieson, top page 124; Jim Bathie, top left page 104; Mary-Gray Hunter, page 43.
Art: Don Smith, Steve Logan, David Morrison
Production: Jerry Higdon

My very special thanks to Carole Austin, Jody House, Diana Leone, Nancy Papa, Yvonne Porcella, Marion Sanders, and Bea Slater for their help in collecting the clothing for this book. Special thanks to Donna Wilder for suggestions on batting. Finally, my warmest appreciation to all the designers who shared their talents—JRL.